TALL LAW

when "trying hard to do better" isn't good enough

S T E V E N   B .   C U R I N G T O N

REFORMERS UNANIMOUS INTERNATIONAL
PO Box 15732, Rockford, IL 61132

Visit our website at www.reformu.com.

Printed in Canada

Cover design by Jeremy Jones, Rockford, IL

Curington, Steven B., 1965-
Tall Law: *When "Trying Hard To Do Better" Isn't Good Enough*
Steven Curington.
ISBN 0-9761498-0

DEDICATION

This book is dedicated to my friend in ministry, Dr. Eric Capaci, who in 2003 challenged me to write something that would help "keep Christian school kids from going bad." He suggested to me that my life experiences after my Christian education and upbringing could have an even more profound influence on young developing teens than it has had on the addicted adults of America.

Thanks for the encouragement, Eric. This represents my best effort at putting together a package of truths that represent what I wish I had learned back when I was a teen. I hope this helps our kids.

CONTENTS

BEHAVIOR MODIFICATION

"Trying Hard To Do Better"

chapter one

CHANGING BEHAVIOR

BEHAVIORAL MODIFICATION. It's just a fancy way of saying someone needs to change the way they're acting. The need for such a change is evident everywhere around us. Take a look at the obnoxious child in the grocery store aisle throwing a fit because his mother won't buy him Super Sugar Shakies for breakfast.

See the disgruntled employee spreading the poison of gossip through the workplace. Consider the corporate executive whose unchecked greed leads him to charge the business for personal expenses even though he makes $2 million a year. Look at the drug dealer giving out free samples to potential customers. There is no doubt that our behavior is in great need of modification. Indeed, it seems that proper behavior is a vanishing character trait that almost qualifies for the endangered species list.

As a society, we are desperately trying to find methods to help us modify unacceptable behavior. Schools hire psychologists to counsel troubled children. New prisons are being built at an amazing rate. Police forces are being expanded. Yet crime remains a problem. The Department of Justice reported in 2004 that more than 2.1 million people were in local, state and federal prisons. Yet crimes continue to be committed in schools, in our communities, in homes, and even in prisons. We have parents killing parents, parents killing kids, kids killing parents, and kids killing other kids.

There is much interest in behavioral modification. Social scientists publish a magazine called Behavior Modification, containing articles that purport to tell people how to control their own behavior as well as that of others. Almost everyone recognizes that there is a need for change in the way people live and act. You can even get advice on how to modify the behavior of your cat from the Animal Protection Institute!

Sadly the problem of bad behavior is found in churches as well. In March of 2005, a church member walked into his church in Wisconsin, pulled out a gun, and began shooting. Before shooting himself, he killed seven people, including the pastor and his wife.

As I travel and speak in Christian high schools and colleges, I find that even their leadership is trying every imaginable method in order to shape the behavior of their Christian young people. Unfortunately, Christians often use the same methods the unsaved world does to modify behavior. Usually they are relying on a system of management that is intended to cause

THE DEPARTMENT OF JUSTICE REPORTED IN 2004 THAT MORE THAN 2.1 MILLION PEOPLE WERE IN LOCAL, STATE AND FEDERAL PRISONS. YET CRIMES CONTINUE TO BE COMMITTED IN SCHOOLS, IN OUR COMMUNITIES, IN HOMES, AND EVEN IN PRISONS.

people to look right, act right, feel right and live right. This system of management is usually a set of laws, steps or rules that are designed to bring behavioral change.

Such a system, however, can only produce dead works! Any system of management whose primary purpose is to produce behavior change is a system that is based on "trying hard to do better." Because of our sinful natures, we always fail when we try in our own strength. So no matter how hard we try, in fact, the harder we try, the more we seem to fail. As a result of this "trying hard" mentality, we are frustrating the spirits of young people in our Christian schools. I know, because I was one of them!

This places us in a quandary. God has called each of us as His children to bring forth fruit—to reproduce ourselves. His calling is for us to recreate the life of Christ in every person in society today and disciple them to be fruit bearing, victorious Christians. But how can we possibly change the behavior of hardened lost people or backslidden believers struggling with habitual sin if we ourselves cannot gain victory over our own inappropriate behavior? If we are selfish, possession-oriented, defeated and frustrated, we cannot share the victorious life with others.

God must have a better plan than a "trying hard" system of management—and He does! It's not man's plan, it's His plan. I want to show you the difference between God's plan for behavioral modification and man's plan. To do that, we must first understand the basic foundational truths of behavioral modification. We'll look at how God created man to function, and expose the devil's alternative to God's plan.

We'll see how Satan lures people away from God and His system of management. I'll walk you through the process by which God enlightens people to that deception and brings them back into His system. We'll see how faith plays a vital role in this process. Finally, we'll conclude with the understanding of how following God's system results in a completely enjoyable life and liberty from besetting sins, despite any and all opposition the enemy brings your way.

chapter two

GOD'S SYSTEM OF MANAGEMENT

"And the Lord God formed man of the dust of the ground, and breathed into his nostrils the breath of life; and man became a living soul."—Genesis 2:7

THE STORY OF CREATION OF MANKIND SHEDS LIGHT ON HOW GOD CREATED MAN TO FUNCTION. The phrase "the dust of the ground" refers to God's creation of our physical bodies. The skin that covers our bodies is called the epidermis. I was teaching this lesson once and I said, "God created the epidural" instead of the "epidermis." When everyone started laughing, I realized the mistake and corrected it. However, my wife did tell me later that God created the epidural too!

After He created man's physical body, God "breathed into his nostrils the breath of life." Whenever we find the phrase "God breathed" in the Bible, it is always talking about a work of the Holy Spirit. God's Spirit was placed within man, and created life. From the beginning, man's spirit was alive. It contained the life of God.

Finally we see the conclusion of creation in the phrase "man became a living soul." The soul is collectively made up of your mind, your will, and your emotions. It is what you think, what you want and what you feel. The soul is what makes up your personality. A fully-functioning human being is made up of three parts in the image of God. This is God's design for man. Let's examine these three parts of man and the way God designed them to function.

Our Spirit. The spirit is the part of man that communicates with God. John 4:24 says, "God is a spirit: and they that worship him must worship him in spirit and in truth." God's intention at creation was to give direction to the spirit of man, and for the spirit to rule over the soul and the body. The function of the spirit of man was to be the master. "Master" comes from the Old English word *maegester*, meaning "one having control or authority." Perhaps the best modern equivalent would be an employer. God intended to be like a silent owner who would not define duties to the body or instruct the soul

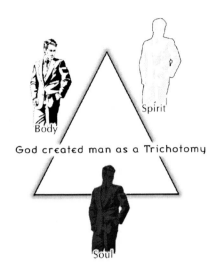

God created man as a Trichotomy

in how to carry those duties out. Instead he would give direction to the spirit of man—the employer. Acting as a good employer would, the spirit then gives direction to his soul.

Our Soul. The soul is the part of man that God intended to take direction from the spirit. For man to fulfill God's purpose, he needed strong desires, proper thinking, and balanced feelings. The soul is a gift from God—the ability to think, to want, and to feel make up our personality, and are good things that allow us to properly discern the best way to carry out the directives we receive in our spirit from the Spirit of God. Thus if the spirit plays the role of the master or employer, the soul fills the role of a steward. The Old English word *stigweard* literally means "house guard." In the 1300's, it began to be used for a person "who manages affairs of an estate on behalf of his employer." The modern equivalent of a steward is a manager. He does not own the business, nor does he make the most important decisions. His responsibility is to carry out his employer's wishes to the best of his ability. To accomplish those results, he gives orders to his employees.

Our Body. The body, according to God's design is act as the servant. The word servant came to English from the French word *servir*, which means "one who attends or waits on another." The best modern equivalent would be an employee. Thus the body is to work as an employee carrying out the commands of the manager (the soul) doing what the employer (the spirit) instructs. These tasks are to be carried out according to instructions. The body follows the will of God by following God's ordained authority within man. Just as a worker who disobeys orders to do what he thinks is right creates chaos in a business setting, for the body to dictate to the soul and spirit violates God's order and brings sin and wrong behavior into life.

God's plan for His creation was that man would function as a spirit-led trichotomy. The spirit rules the soul and the soul instructs and manages the body. That was the way Adam and Eve began in the Garden of Eden. Since Adam was functioning as God intended, God was able to instruct his spirit. He began by telling Adam what he should do, what he should not do, and what would happen if he failed to obey what God had commanded to his spirit.

God's System of Management for Man

God

SPIRIT
Communicates with God
(Stimulates intuition,
worship, and conscience)

SOUL
Yields to God's Communicated Will
using his mind, will, emotions

God's Will

BODY
Receives direction from the soul
(Carries out God's will)

chapter three

MEASURED FREEDOM

*"And the Lord God took the man, and put him into the garden of Eden to dress it and to keep it. And the Lord God commanded the man, saying, Of every tree of the garden thou mayest **freely** eat: **But** of the tree of the knowledge of good and evil, thou shalt not eat of it: for in the day that thou eatest thereof thou shalt surely die."* —Genesis 2:15-17

GOD NEVER LEAVES US WITHOUT DIRECTION. From the very beginning of creation, He gave Adam a job to perform. Adam was to dress the Garden of Eden and keep it. God also placed boundaries on Adam's behavior. He told Adam what he could and could not do. God gave Adam permission to eat from any of the trees in the garden. That's freedom. However, after telling Adam that, God followed the gift of freedom with a restriction. He told Adam he could not eat from 'the tree of the knowledge of good and evil.

That seems somewhat contradictory. If you are giving someone freedom, why follow that with restrictions? The reason this seems contradictory is that most people do not truly understand what freedom is and how it works. You see, freedom is measured by its boundaries.

I found this truth out the hard way. I was raised in a Christian home and attended Christian school. I remember the days when I couldn't wait to get out from under all those rules! The rules seemed so restrictive. I felt they were keeping me in bondage—at least that's what I thought at the time. I would even say, "Once I graduate and move out, I'm going to break loose from all these rules and regulations and really be free." What I did not realize then is that anytime you violate God's boundaries, you only exchange your boundaries for bondage.

Freedom is only found within God's boundaries. Every time you step outside those boundaries, you are placing yourself in bondage. There are no freedoms anywhere in life that do not have boundaries attached to them.

When my wife and I had Charity, our first child, we did not trust her very much. As a result, we did not allow her to drive the car. As a matter of fact, that little baby had very little freedom. She received her freedom inside a little box that we placed her in. In that box, she was free to eat, sleep, play, cry—sometimes she even went to the bathroom in that box. The box had bars like a prison, but of course it was really a crib. Charity had complete freedom within that crib.

As she grew, we gave her more freedom. We placed her inside a bigger box. It had netting instead of bars. Just as she was inside the first box, she was free to eat, sleep, play and cry. And she still went to the bathroom in her playpen. She enjoyed complete freedom as long as she stayed within the confines of that playpen.

When she started to walk, we gave her more freedom. She now could move around within the house. Of course she couldn't handle the stairs alone, so we placed boundaries (little gates) at the top and bottom of the stairs. Outside of that, however, she had the freedom of the house. As long as she observed the boundaries we had established, she had much greater freedom than before.

At the time I'm writing this, Charity is nine. She now has had her freedoms extended again. She will come to my wife and say, "Mom, can I go outside?" Usually Lori will reply "Yes, as long as you stay in the yard." Her freedom has now expanded all the way out to the edge of the fence in the backyard.

The next measure of freedom hasn't come to her yet, but I well remember when I received the freedom of the neighborhood. I would ask my mother if I could ride my bike over to Dominic's house. She would often reply, "Go ahead, but be sure you stay in the neighborhood." I had my freedom expanded. Then one day my father was driving home from work and saw me a few blocks away at Greg's house. It was back to the yard for me. And if I gave him any lip, it was back in the house. If I wasn't careful, I'd end up back in the crib! Freedom is enjoyed and enlarged when boundaries are respected and obeyed. Yet those freedoms are eliminated when they are not.

Then the greatest day in my life arrived—at least I thought so at the time. My father walked into the room and tossed me the keys to his

1979 Chrysler Grenada. (Why are you laughing?) But not long after that key toss, I looked up one day as I was driving and saw colored lights flashing in the rear view mirror. That didn't happen just once, or even twice, but three times in the first year I had my license! I learned that I can't drive….fifty-five! Because of my inability to remain within the boundaries of my new freedom by obeying the rules of the road, I lost that freedom. For six months, it was back to the bike!

True freedom is always measured by its boundaries, not by the absence of boundaries. The choice you make to either respect those boundaries or not is the difference between true freedom and bondage. God told Adam not to eat of the tree of the knowledge of good and evil. That tree was in the middle of the garden, and it represented the only boundary in Adam's world. The fruit of that tree offered man the ability to be led from a source other than God. The wrong choice would give the mind, will and emotions of man—his soul—the desire to think, want and feel things that were different from God's design.

TRUE FREEDOM IS ALWAYS MEASURED BY ITS BOUNDARIES, NOT BY THE ABSENCE OF BOUNDARIES. THE CHOICE YOU MAKE TO EITHER RESPECT THOSE BOUNDARIES OR NOT IS THE DIFFERENCE BETWEEN TRUE FREEDOM AND BONDAGE.

We could call that tree the "tree of information." The knowledge that could be gained by eating the fruit would make man like God. That's what the devil told Eve, and as he often does, he was using part of the truth to sell his deception. The difference is that the tree of information would make man like God in his own power rather than in God's power. God does want us to be like Him, but He wants us to do it according to His design—to be like Him in His power.

God was so strongly against man abusing his freedom and choosing to eat from the tree that He told Adam that "in the day" that he did, he would "surely die." There was no uncertainly or ambiguity about God's instruction to Adam. God initially gave this instruction to Adam. In fact, Eve had not yet been created when God issued His command against eating the fruit of the tree. We know that God held Eve responsible for obeying it, because she was punished when she violated the commandment.

It is quite likely that Eve's failure to remember the details of what God actually instructed was a direct result of her husband failing to accurately teach her God's words. When the subtle serpent came to tempt her to sin, she did not reject his temptation. As a result, the measured freedom God had given to man had its boundaries violated. That violation was caused by an outside pressure that took advantage of Eve's weak personal relationship with God. I call that outside pressure the "devil's system of management."

chapter four

THE DEVIL'S SYSTEM OF MANAGEMENT

"Love not the world, neither the things that are in the world. If any man love the world, the love of the Father is not in him. For all that is in the world, the lust of the flesh, and the lust of the eyes, and the pride of life, is not of the Father, but is of the world."—I John 2:15-16

THE DEVIL'S DESIRE FROM THE BEGINNING WAS TO CORRUPT THE RELATIONSHIP GOD ENJOYED WITH HIS HUMAN CREATION. His means of doing this was offering man an alternative to God's system of management that we looked at in the last chapter. The primary difference between the devil's system and God's system is in the location of the influence.

God's system is based on inward persuasion. The inner man (the spirit) directs the outer man (the soul) to carry out God's will for his life. The devil's system is based on outside pressure. His plan was to use outside pressures to gain control of man's soul. The soul is where the gift of freedom dwells. Thus if the devil succeeded in using outside pressure to cause man's soul to reject God's system of internal persuasion, Satan could gain control of God's creation. The means the devil uses to attack our souls is called temptation.

The devil's management system is laid out very clearly in the verses at the beginning of this chapter. In these verses we see the means by which he uses temptation to stimulate the mind or direct the will or effect the emotions of man to influence him to reject God's system of internal persuasion. John describes in these verses the world system that is being used by Satan to pull us away from God.

The first thing that we see emphasized in the verses is the exclusive nature of the two systems. You cannot love the world and love God at the same time. In fact, John indicates that loving the world shows that we do not have God's love within us. There are three particular desires that make up a love of the world—the lust of the flesh, the lust of the eyes, and the pride of life. Each of these is targeted at a specific part of the soul in the devil's attempt to draw us away from God and into his outward system of management.

First, we see **the lust of the flesh**. This could be defined as **a consuming desire to *do***. If a person could do anything he wanted from the day he was born until the day he died, he would gain one third of the world. The lust of the flesh is a temptation that is primarily directed against the mind. In the mind, we think of things that we would like to do. It's important to realize that these things may not in and of themselves be wrong. Satan tried to get Jesus to turn stones into bread. There is nothing intrinsically wrong with bread.

But anything that we do apart from God's purpose, plan or persuasion is sinful. The devil doesn't have to get you to do something completely sinful to cause you to fall. He simply needs to lead you to yield to your own desires instead of God's. The other thing to remember is that no one gets to do everything they want to do. And even if you somehow could, you would still have only "gained" one third of what the world has to offer. There would still be two thirds left.

> **THE DEVIL DOESN'T HAVE TO GET YOU TO DO SOMETHING COMPLETELY SINFUL TO CAUSE YOU TO FALL. HE SIMPLY NEEDS TO LEAD YOU TO YIELD TO YOUR OWN DESIRES INSTEAD OF GOD'S.**

Second, we see **the lust of the eyes**. This could be defined as a **compelling urge to *have***. The lust of the eyes is aimed at our will. Through the lust of the eyes, the devil tries to gain influence over our wills by filling us with the desire to acquire. We live in an advertising culture dedicated to creating a level of dissatisfaction that will move us to purchase whatever product they are selling.

Again, it is not having things that is wrong; it is when things have us that we have fallen into Satan's trap. The devil showed Jesus all the kingdoms of the world in an attempt to divert Him from God's plan for His life. Things that you acquire apart from God's means are sinful, even if they are not wrong in and of themselves. A person who got everything they ever wanted to have would still only have "gained" one third of what the world had to offer. There would still be one third left.

Finally, we see **the pride of life**. This could be defined as a **conceited drive to be**. Almost everyone struggles with what they want to be at some point in his life. It's not so much that we don't want to be what God wants us to be as it is we hope He wants us to be what we want to be! There is a great deal of pressure on people today to achieve something notable by the world's standards. The pride of life is primarily a temptation aimed at our emotions.

Satan tempted Jesus by encouraging Him to jump from the pinnacle of the temple and be dramatically rescued by angels in front of the people. This would establish His reputation forever. Understanding who God wants us to be protects us from the outside pressures of the pride of life.

When I was a child, I wanted to be a fireman. That desire was not because God was leading me in that direction, but because I had seen a movie about firemen. When I got a little older, I wanted to play baseball. I watched Ryan Sandberg play second base for the Cubs on WGN, and I had a great desire to become a baseball player. There was even a phase in my life when I wanted to be a Marine. The main reason I wanted to be a Marine was because their dress uniforms were so cool!

These are all examples of outside pressures influencing career decisions. There is nothing wrong with encouraging people to be all they can be. I want my children to grow and learn and excel. The danger comes when we replace the internal persuasion of the Spirit of God with external pressures (parents, teachers, friends, sometimes even pastors) that are not in keeping with God's plan.

God told Adam to dress the Garden of Eden and keep it. That was His purpose for Adam's life. Eve was directed to "help meet" Adam's needs. Satan came with a much more tempting offer. He told

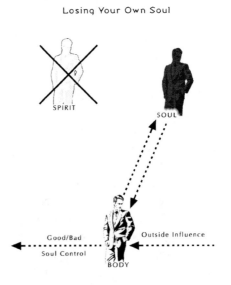

Losing Your Own Soul

SPIRIT

SOUL

Good/Bad
Soul Control

Outside Influence

BODY

Eve that if she ate of the fruit of the tree of knowledge of good and evil, she would be like God. The outside pressure from the devil influenced Adam and Eve to trade in God's purpose for something "better."

If you got to do all you ever wanted to do, you would have "gained" the final one third of the world. So if you had everything you wanted to have and did everything you wanted to do and were everything you wanted to be, you would have "gained" the whole world. The problem is that the world would have your soul as well. Jesus said, "For what shall it profit a man, if he shall gain the whole world, and lose his own soul?" (Mark 8:36)

Now most of us recognize that if a man's primary focus is on pleasing himself throughout life, and as a result he never accepts Christ as Savior, that man will lose his soul and spend eternity in hell. But wait a minute! I know a lot of Christians (included me at times) who dwell on doing what they want, demand to have what they want, and get depressed if they don't get to be what they want to be. Too many Christians have an undue affection for the things of the world. In a sense, those Christians lose their soul. Not for eternity, for the soul that trusts Christ as Savior is saved for certain and for ever.

But it is possible for a Christian to yield "control of his soul" to the devil when we give in to these external pressures. That's right. Yielding to outside pressure, that is to act in rebellion to internal persuasion, will cause us to lose "control" of our soul.

God's system of management, whereby He communicates internal persuasion to our spirit ensures that we follow His will. God's will is not some mystical, hard to understand, nebulous thing. It is simply for our lives to be made up only of what He wants us to do, to be, and to have. When the outside pressure of the devil persuades us to seek fulfillment apart from God's will, he gains a foothold of control over our soul.

Eventually, if we do not deal with the problem, the foothold will become a stronghold. Strongholds are positions of power that we give to the devil by yielding to his outside pressure. They bind us in chains that slow our productivity for God. Sampson is a great example of this process. Because he gave in to Satan's pressure to fulfill his appetites and gain glory for himself apart from God's will, he ended up bound with chains by the Philistines.

If you still do not deal with your sin, it will finally become a stranglehold that will allow the devil to completely destroy your availability to be used by God. At that point Satan has gained control over your soul. You are still Heaven bound, but you are going to get there the hard way. This condition is what we call demonic oppression. Oppression is simply another word to describe outside pressures attempting to gain control of your soul.

chapter five

THE FALL OF MAN

"Now the serpent was more subtil than any beast of the field which the Lord God had made. And he said unto the woman, Yea, hath God said, Ye shall not eat of every tree of the garden? And the woman said unto the serpent, We may eat of the fruit of the trees of the garden: But of the fruit of the tree which is in the midst of the garden, God hath said, Ye shall not eat of it, neither shall ye touch it, lest ye die. And the serpent said unto the woman, Ye shall not surely die: For God doth know that in the day ye eat thereof, then your eyes shall be opened, and ye shall be as gods, knowing good and evil."—Genesis 3:1-7

TO UNDERSTAND THE FULL IMPACT OF THE FALL OF MAN, YOU MUST FIRST UNDERSTAND THE STATE IN WHICH MAN WAS CREATED. Many people assume that Adam was created perfect and holy. That is not correct. Adam was created innocent. He was neither holy, nor unholy. As a result of his innocent state, no modification of his behavior was needed. He was completely submissive to God's management system—internal persuasion. Adam's spirit governed his soul and his body according to the directives he had received from God.

What we see described in Genesis chapter three is the first conflict between God's internal system of management and Satan's external system. As we look at this conflict, it's important to realize what was going on. For the first time, outside pressure from the devil was brought to bear on Adam and Eve. Satan's goal was to get man to disobey what God had commanded. If he could succeed, he would gain control over the soul of man.

Satan used the things of the world—the lust of the flesh, the lust of the eyes, and the pride of life—that we discussed in the last chapter to accomplish his purpose. The Bible says "the tree was good for food", which appealed to the lust of the flesh. The tree was "pleasant to the eyes," appealing to the lust of the eyes. Finally, the tree was "to be desired to make one wise," appealing to the pride of life. These outside pressures influenced Eve to exercise her freedom of choice and disobey God's direct command.

The external influence won the battle, and Eve took the fruit of the tree and ate it. For the first time, her behavior was governed by her soul rather than by her spirit. You will not obey God unless you are under control of your spirit, listening to His Spirit. By following the dictates of her soul—her mind, her will, and her emotions—she violated the boundary God had set for her and her husband.

Satan secured control over Eve's soul by the outside influences he used against her. Once he had gained that control, he could manipulate her behavior just like you would use a joystick to control a video game. By using all three elements of the world, Satan relocated Eve's control from her spirit to her soul. When you are focused on what you want to have, what you want to do, and what you want to be rather than on God's purpose for your life, your soul is under the devil's control. It may not be satanic possession, but it is none the less satanic oppression—outside pressure.

By using the things of the world to tempt each portion of our soul, the devil is working to get us to abandon God's system of management. If you allow him to gain dominance over any portion of your soul by yielding to outside pressure, you have given him a position from which to govern your behavior.

In the case of Eve, her failure began with the lust of the flesh. Her mind dwelled on the appearance of the fruit. She decided that it would be good for food, despite the fact that God had specifically commanded that the fruit from that tree not be eaten. As she thought and meditated on it, the attractiveness of the fruit outweighed her commitment to obedience. Dr. Bob Jones, Sr. used to say, "Behind every tragedy of human character is a long process of wicked thinking."

Then the lust of the eyes began to impact and compel her will. She began to covet and desire something that she knew she was not supposed to have. If you allow your appetites for things you know are wrong to be your focus, you will find a way to fulfill that appetite. That's why the Apostle Paul said, "Make not provision for the flesh, to fulfil the lusts thereof." (Rom. 13:14) The moment Eve contemplated to reach out and take the fruit of the tree, she lost control of her soul.

Finally the devil used the pride of life. He told Eve that eating the fruit would make her like God, "knowing good and evil." By the way, she already knew good! She knew God. He was as much good as she would ever need to know. The only thing she got out of her bargain with the devil was to know evil. That knowledge came from the one who was now in control of her soul.

She wanted to be something God did not mean for her to be. Her emotional response to a good thing (being like God) overwhelmed her judgment against using a bad means to a good end. You never please God by doing what He has commanded you not to do, regardless of what your motive is.

Of course Satan was not content with merely deceiving Eve. He will never stop until he has destroyed everything that he can. His real focus was to gain control over Adam. The Bible does not tell us how Adam responded to Eve's mistake. It simply says that when Eve gave him the fruit, "he did eat." The devil used the same tactic of outside pressure to gain control over Adam.

The means of the outside pressure was Eve. She gave Adam the fruit. Of course he knew that what she had done was wrong. God's commandment had been very clear. Adam knew Eve had violated God's boundaries. He also knew the consequences God had set down—that she would die. He may have reasoned within himself that if she were taken from him, he would be alone again.

Adam also allowed his soul to overrule his spirit, and he ate the forbidden fruit. When sin entered the soul, man was plunged into darkness. In the Bible,

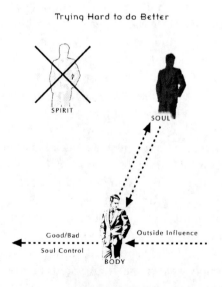

Trying Hard to do Better

SPIRIT

SOUL

Good/Bad
Soul Control

Outside Influence

BODY

darkness is a symbol of lack of spiritual direction. By violating God's boundaries, man incurred the death penalty. It is true that physical death entered the world with the fall, but in examining God's response to Adam's sin, we see another kind of death as well.

God said to Adam, "Because thou has harkened unto the voice of thy wife and hast eaten of the tree." Notice that God is identifying the point at which Adam succumbed to Satan's external system. Rather than listening to God's voice speaking to his spirit, he listened to the voice of his wife. He yielded to her outside pressure instead of to God's command, and allowed it to govern his behavior. Forced to choose between the internal control of the spirit and the external control of the devil working through his wife, Adam chose to do something he knew was wrong.

> **DR. BOB JONES, SR. USED TO SAY, "BEHIND EVERY TRAGEDY OF HUMAN CHARACTER IS A LONG PROCESS OF WICKED THINKING."**

Then notice God's reaction. He said, "Cursed is the ground for thy sake; in sorrow thou shalt eat of it all the days of thy life." (Gen. 3:17) This seems to contradict what God had first told Adam. He said that in the day Adam ate the fruit, he would "surely die." (Gen. 2:17) Did God change His mind on the punishment for sin? Did He lie when He told man he would die? Not at all. God always keeps His word.

Something did die that day in the Garden of Eden... the spirit of man died! With a dead spirit, man could no longer hear from God internally. He was plunged into darkness, unable to discern the proper spiritual direction to follow. Without the personal relationship he had once enjoyed with God, walking in fellowship daily, man set out to "try" to do good in his *own* power.

From the day that sin entered into the soul until now, man has been desperately searching for a way to modify his behavior. Sometimes it worked, as was the case with Abel, and sometimes it did not, as was the case with Cain. Thus man began his own plan to modify his behavior. He would "try hard to do better." He would do good in his own power.

To do this, his body would react to good or bad external pressure and dictate to the soul the direction he wanted to go. The soul, using his mind, will, or emotions, would attempt to discern if the outside pressure was good or bad. If it was good he would yield to it, and "do good in his own power." If he didn't care one way or another, he would simply yield to the desires of his body. Of course, our body in its now corrupt nature housed sin in its members. (See chart at left.) Thus we would eventually require an enforcing authority to get us to act right and to reject the wrong desires of the body.

chapter six

BEHAVIOR MODIFICATION —MAN'S PLAN

THE ONLY OPTION AVAILABLE TO MAN TO GOVERN HIS BEHAVIOR AFTER THE DEATH OF HIS SPIRIT WAS PERSONAL SOUL CONTROL. The only way he could do good was in his own strength and power. Man's soul, apart from the direction of his spirit, could be easily drawn away from doing good by outside pressures. Even if man's soul desired to do good, he could not necessarily determine what was good or bad.

Since his spirit was dead, he could no longer communicate with God. This rendered him vulnerable to the outside influences the devil used to draw him away from good behavior. Even worse, because sin had entered into his body, it now had the power to control him. He was under the power of sin. Romans 5:12 says, "Wherefore, as by one man sin entered into the world, and death by sin; and so death passed upon all men, for that all have sinned:"

The soul naturally yields to the negotiations of the sinful body. That is the definition of what the Bible calls "walking after the flesh." Many people think that walking according to the flesh means all kinds of wicked behavior. But the true definition is simply the soul's willingness to be led by the body rather than by the spirit.

When Satan brings his outside pressures to bear on man, the sin in our body desires to give in to the temptation and yield to the pressure. Oscar Wilde, who was not exactly known for moral behavior, once said, "I can resist anything except temptation." The body cannot yield to sin without first gaining the cooperation of the soul. Thus the body negotiates with the soul to get it to think, feel, and choose to do what it wants to do.

The only way for man in this condition to do good is to control or minimize the outside pressures and temptations. Of course as Jesus taught us in the Lord's Prayer, God is in control of when we are led into temptation. That means that outside pressures and temptation are not under our control. Since sin lead us out from under God's control, our ability to behave properly has been greatly hindered.

In response, man developed a plan and a system to behave properly and to modify improper behavior. The goal of this plan was to learn to be like God *in our own power*. If this sounds familiar, that's because it's exactly the temptation the devil used to deceive Eve in the Garden of Eden.

In order to become more like God and do good, we needed to know more about God. However, without a living spirit capable of receiving communication from the creator, man was not able to learn about Him. We didn't know enough about God to be able to act like God, no matter what level of self-discipline we were able to muster up.

Eventually men tried to build the tower at Babel. In part, the purpose behind that project was to reach up to the heavens so that man could hear from God. Every effort man made failed miserably. In fact the Bible says in Genesis 6:5 that "every imagination of the thoughts of his heart was only evil continually." God sent the flood to destroy man, saving only the righteous remnant of Noah and his family.

All through our history, we have thought that the more we know, the better off we will be. We have been taught that the acquisition of information will lead to the power to behave properly. If you're of a certain age, you probably remember the Schoolhouse Rock cartoons on Saturday mornings. Their message was "Knowledge Is Power!" No, its not! Knowing Him is power! The problem is that such a message, while it appeals to our intellect, is false. Dr. Bob Jones, Sr. used to say, "Education without God makes men clever devils."

In the Garden of Eden, Adam and Eve enjoyed a dynamic walk with God every day. They had an intimate, personal relationship with Him. They knew Him, and He knew them. But when they decided to eat of the forbidden fruit, what they were really saying was that the tree of "information" had more to offer them than God did. They chose the acquisition of information over the development of a personal relation with God. They settled for knowing about God instead of really knowing God.

Man's thirst for information about God was driven by the realization that we could not be like God without knowing what God is like. After thousands of years, God finally gave man a tool to help him do what was right. Given the futility of trying to do good in our own strength, we had to have help. God's plan was to offer an alternative to man's efforts to do good on his own. So God gave the Law. The word law means "a rule of conduct."

The Law was a set of rules, steps, and boundaries that man could follow to produce a behavioral change. God gave the Law to a specially chosen group of people—the nation of Israel. Following the Law of God had a profound impact on the behavior of God's chosen people, particularly when it was enforced by the spiritual leadership of the country.

IT IS IMPORTANT TO REMEMBER THAT GOD'S PLAN WAS NOT TO PROVIDE A SET OF RULES THAT MAN COULD KEEP. THE LAW WAS A SET OF RULES THAT COULD NEVER BE KEPT.

It's interesting to note that the laws that governed the nation of Israel were sometimes intentionally adopted, at least in part, by other countries. When those nations followed the Law of God, even without the covenant relationship that Israel enjoyed, they saw the barbaric behavior of their citizens become more civilized. An effective system for the management of mankind was essential for civilization to develop.

Man then used the standard which he knew had come from God as a standard for his attempt to try to become like God. It is important to remember that God's plan was not to provide a set of rules that man could keep. The law was a set of rules that could never be kept. God knew that, not matter how hard man tried to keep the Law in his own strength, he would always fail. In fact, the harder we try, the more we fail.

The effort to become righteous in our own power only brings condemnation. The Law condemns us for even the smallest violation. Our efforts to experience liberty over the body of sin only served to demonstrate that sin did indeed have power over us. Life under the Law was incredibly frustrating.

We are truly blessed that we did not live under the Law. For thousands of years, people did not hear directly from God. I Samuel 3:1 says, "And the child Samuel ministered unto the LORD before Eli. And the word of the LORD was precious in those days; there was no open vision." Occasionally God would speak to a prophet or send a messenger to bring a communication from Him. But information from an intermediary is a far cry from a personal, intimate relationship with God like Adam and Eve had in the Garden of Eden.

All man had was a set of rules by which to conform himself in his own strength. That effort was doomed to fail. The only relief from the frustration of trying to keep the Law was the hope that God had given for the future. The future hope was that the Messiah would come and bring deliverance. That is why the angel told Joseph, "And she shall bring forth a son, and thou shalt call his name JESUS: for he shall save his people from their sins." (Matt. 1:21) God planned to redeem the soul of man and restore his spirit-led trichotomy.

chapter seven

BEHAVIOR MODIFICATION —GOD'S PLAN

GOD DID NOT INTEND TO LEAVE MAN DEPENDENT ON THE FRUSTRATION OF TRYING TO KEEP THE LAW IN ORDER TO MODIFY HIS BEHAVIOR. Accordingly He sent a second Adam. Throughout the acquisition of information age, this coming was foretold by many prophets. The nation of Israel believed the promises that had been made to them. In his sermon on the day of Pentecost, Peter said, "For the promise is unto you, and to your children, and to all that are afar off, even as many as the Lord our God shall call." (Acts 2:39)

The second Adam—Jesus—had a living Spirit. Thus He lived His life as God had designed all men to live, in constant internal communication with God. As a result, He rejected soul control and lived according to Spirit control. He said, "I do always those things that please him." (John 8:29)

Although Jesus was fully God, He did not live a perfect life as God. That would have had no value for us, for we could not replicate it. He lived a perfect life as a Spirit-led man. Thus he provided an example for us that we can emulate. When we talk about being Christ-like, we are simply talking about living "like" Christ lived.

In order for that to happen, our soul must first be redeemed by the precious blood of Jesus. The Bible teaches us that when we are saved, the Spirit of Truth—the Holy Spirit—comes to dwell within us. (John 16:7) At that point we have the means to live an internally led life.

But even though we have the potential, we must yearn and learn to yield to the influence of God's Spirit. If we do, we will develop spiritually and experience the power of the crucified Christian life. First, we must die so that Christ can live through us. Christ did not die to change my life; He died so that He could exchange my life! Paul said, "For to me to live is Christ, and to die is gain." (Phil. 1:21)

God's plan allows us to be like Christ in His power rather than in our own. One of the most familiar verses in the Bible is John 3:16. "For God so loved the world, that he gave his only begotten Son, that whosoever believeth in him should not perish, but have everlasting life." While this verse is well known, people often miss the teaching that is contains about our new life in Christ.

John 3:16 teaches us that, through the substitutionary death of Jesus Christ, we are offered eternal life. Most people use this verse to teach that those who believe on Christ as Savior have Heaven awaiting them. While this is true, the verse teaches much more than that. Our eternal destiny in Heaven is secured, but that is only one of the benefits of salvation.

Salvation includes the benefits of both justification and sanctification. These concepts are often misunderstood, or the terms are used incorrectly. Justification is freedom from the penalty of sin—death and Hell. Through Christ's death and our faith in Him, we escape that penalty. That is why the verse says "whosoever believeth in him should not perish." Sanctification is freedom from the power of sin. This is found in the phrase "but have everlasting life."

Everlasting life is not teaching us that when we die we live forever in Heaven. Since we will not perish, we will never die. Oh our heart will stop beating and our body will die, but our spirit will not. Our spirit comes alive when we accept Christ as our personal Savior. Our everlasting life does not begin when the body dies and we go to Heaven; it begins the moment you are saved.

By definition, everlasting life means life in perpetuity. If does not begin at our physical death, but at our second birth. This life in the spirit exists while we live on earth and continues through eternity in Heaven. As a child of God, you have the privilege of enjoying immediate eternal existence through the regeneration of your spirit and the indwelling of the Holy Spirit.

We see another picture of these two benefits of salvation in the process of baptism. We are buried with Christ in a picture of His death, symbolizing justification. Then we are raised in Christ as a picture of His resurrection, symbolizing sanctification.

Baptism wouldn't work very well if the preacher held the person under the water and never brought him back up! We are "raised to walk in newness of life." The problem is that many believers do not walk in that new life. Some Christians leave the baptistery and start trying to do good in their own power, just as they did before they were saved. That is not God's plan.

Justification gets you to Heaven, and sanctification allows you to enjoy a little bit of Heaven on Earth! Enjoying the sanctified life and its benefits depends on your willingness to yield to the Holy Spirit living in you. The devil will try to steal your joy by hiding the truth of sanctification from the believer, just as he tries to hide the truth of justification from the unbeliever.

We receive the benefits of justification when we die, but the benefits of sanctification are meant to be enjoyed here and now. We cannot benefit from

ENJOYING THE SANCTIFIED LIFE AND ITS BENEFITS DEPENDS ON YOUR WILLINGNESS TO YIELD TO THE HOLY SPIRIT LIVING IN YOU.

sanctification if we are not willing to follow God's plan and conform to His image. Again, His image for man is a functioning trichotomy. But a functioning trichotomy is not enough; we must be a Spirit-led trichotomy.

This is what the Bible refers to as being a Spirit-led man. The only way for this to happen is for us to learn to enjoy the benefits of sanctification. We cannot live free from the devil's outside pressures unless we are yielding to our sanctification. How and where does the process of sanctification take place? It happens in our previously dead spirit.

The Bible says in Ephesians 2:1, "And you hath he quickened who were dead in trespasses and sins." The word "quickened" means made alive. Nothing can be made alive that is not first dead. We were dead spiritually because of our trespasses. To trespass means to cross a boundary. When Adam and Eve at the forbidden fruit, they crossed the only boundary God had placed on their behavior.

Since it was the spirit that died when sin entered the world, we can conclude that it is man's spirit being made alive again that this verse is talking about. To be more specific, God actually replaces our dead spirit with a new, living spirit. He then fills our living spirit with His Spirit.

This is an amazing miracle of transformation! For thousands of years, the majority of people on the earth—all except those who believed in the coming Messiah—were dead on the inside. Now they could be alive again. There is a prophecy regarding this transformation in the book of Ezekiel.

"A new heart also will I give you, and **a new spirit will I put within you:** and I will take away the stony heart out of your flesh, and I will give you an heart of flesh. And I **will put my spirit within you,** and cause you to walk in my statutes, and ye shall keep my judgments, and do them."—Ezekiel 36:26-27

Notice the effect of God's Spirit indwelling and empowering our new living spirit. We are given the power to walk according to God's statutes and keep His judgments. Because we are now alive on the inside, we can once again communicate with God and have the internal persuasion of His Spirit within. When we yield to this internal persuasion, we can be obedient, vibrant, living Christians.

This is an amazing truth! For a majority of human history, people did not hear from God personally. They were not able to walk with Him in an intimate way. But now the Spirit of God lives within those of us who are His children. Too many of us take this truth for granted. Some people say that the Holy Spirit is a comforter and a convicter. Others say He is an influence or a persuasion. We seldom if ever explain these things to our Christian school kids, much less to our baby, developing Christians.

He is all of those things, but He is much more. The Holy Spirit is a *person* who lives within your spirit. He does not communicate to your soul, He communicates with your spirit—your inner man. He made your spirit alive when you were saved, and as He dwells within you, He seeks to lead and guide you through internal persuasion. Jesus said in John 16:7 and in John 16:13-14:

"Nevertheless I tell you the truth; It is expedient for you that I go away: for if I go not away, the Comforter will not come unto you; but if I depart, I will send him unto you. Howbeit when he, the Spirit of truth, is come, he will guide you into all truth: for he shall not speak of himself; but whatsoever he shall hear, that shall he speak: and he will shew you things to come. He shall glorify me: for he shall receive of mine, and shall shew it to you."—John 16:7, 13-14

Jesus was saying that through the Holy Spirit, He would transmit guidance to us as to how we should live. Did you ever play with walkie-talkies when you were a kid? (Or am I giving away my age?) They allowed you to talk to your friends, even if they were a few houses away. In the same way, The Holy Spirit is God's "Walkie-Talkie" and He allows us to receive God's direction in our spirits.

Likewise, when we pray, we may use that same communication with God. Romans 8:26 says "The Spirit itself maketh intercession for us with groanings that cannot be uttered." The Bible calls this praying in the Spirit. We have the basis now for a personal, intimate relationship with God, just like Adam and Eve enjoyed in the garden before the fall. I refer to this as the restoration of a personal relation age, which replaced the acquisition of information age.

With the Spirit leading and offering guidance to our living spirit, our submissive soul can direct our body to obey God as a functioning trichotomy. We now have the opportunity to reject soul control and choose spirit control instead. The inner man can lead rather than the outer man. This only happens as we choose Christ's crucified life over our own selfish choices.

That level of submission will modify our behavior, not as a result of acquiring information but through the development of a personal relation with God. The advantage of this kind of behavior modification is that, because it is according to God's design, it produces lasting results rather than frustration.

To gain this kind of personal relation with God, we need to understand the value of developing the relationship. We must yield to the inner man. It is not enough to be justified by believing in Jesus' substitutionary death. That belief provides you with a new and living spirit that *may* be used by God through sanctification.

However you will not be used by God if you do not learn to yield to the benefits of the sanctification process. You must be willing to be conformed to the image of God's Son as you yield to His indwelling Spirit. It is not enough to be a trichotomy to overcome the power of the world's outside pressures. You must be a functioning trichotomy with all three parts—body, soul, and spirit—functioning according to God's design.

If any one of the three parts of man does not function according to God's design, the whole life is affected. To achieve His purpose, we must function as a living spirit, a dying soul (dying to self) and a God-glorifying body. The spirit must be in charge of the soul, or in other words, the inner man must lead the outer man.

Because of the sin that is still present in the body, even after salvation, the body will attempt to gain control over the soul and feed its appetites. The soul must remain in subjection to the spirit for man to live a life that is pleasing to God. Thus the internal persuasion overrules the external influences that draw men to sin. The internal persuasion only triumphs when the believer has developed a dynamic love relationship with Jesus Christ.

You must exchange the old system of acquisition of information for the new system of developing a personal relation in order for your inward man to be strengthened. There is no other way for you to enjoy living a God-pleasing life. Such a walk with God gives you the ability to modify your behavior and triumph over sin. Again, it's vital to remember that this cannot be done in your own strength. Trying to do good on your own guarantees frustration and failure.

chapter eight

THE RESTORATION OF A PERSONAL RELATION

AT THIS POINT, WE NEED TO PAUSE TO LOOK AT THE DIFFERENCE BETWEEN ACQUIRING INFORMATION AND BUILDING A PERSONAL RELATION. In saying that the personal relation age replaced the acquiring information age, I am certainly not downplaying the importance of information. Ignorance is not bliss! Not for a moment do I think that a believer should be ignorant about God. But I also do not believe that God intends for us to be primarily information gatherers.

To understand the difference, look back at how God ushered in the age of the restoration of a personal relation. After the fall of man, our confidence was in ourselves. Man went on a search for knowledge about God so that he could be like Him in his own power. That's pride. God hates the sin of pride very much.

One of the reasons God hates pride is that it destroys our ability to have a relationship with Him. Pride damages both sides of our relationship with God. It keeps us from seeking Him, but when we try to come into His presence with pride in our hearts, it repulses God. James 4:6 says, "But he giveth more grace. Wherefore he saith, God resisteth the proud, but giveth grace unto the humble."

God had a plan to rescue our sin sick souls. But He knew that we would not respond to developing a relation in order to heal our fallen state. Adam had rejected that in the Garden. He knew that the only thing we would accept would be information. So God sent a second Adam, His Son Jesus, into the world, to live a perfect life and die and be raised again for our redemption.

Those of us who have accepted this "information" about God's Son for our salvation by faith have been justified. Our souls have been saved from death and Hell. So you see, our justification depends upon the acceptance of acquired information. When we accept Christ's death on the cross by faith, we become believers. But God does not want us to stop there. His plan for us includes much more than justification.

After we are saved, God wants us to move from acquiring more information to developing a personal relation with Him. Although justification comes with the acquiring of information, sanctification never does. We will never experience and enjoy the benefits of sanctification if we do not develop a personal walk with God. Information is simply the fuel that our personal relationship burns as it grows.

To help you understand the distinction, let's focus our attention on the differences between justification and sanctification. The first difference is in our relationship with sin. Justification frees us from the penalty of sin; sanctification frees us from the power of sin. Because of justification, I do have to die and go to Hell to pay for my sins. Because of sanctification, I do not have to live daily under the dominion of sin.

Romans 6:14 says, "For sin shall not have dominion over you: for ye are not under the law, but under grace." Under the law, man did the work in his own power. Under grace, God does all the work. This is a vital point. Many well-meaning, sincere Christians believe that if you want the victory over sin, you must work and do all that you can. That is wrong! That's "trying hard to do better."

The victory over sin has already been won. If you want the victory, stop trying to do things yourself and let God do things for you! Most of you who are reading this understand that we don't do anything to get saved. God does all the justifying. But grace teaches us that He does the sanctifying too!

We cannot sanctify ourselves. The power to triumph over sin does not rest in us. The process of learning to enjoy the benefits of sanctification starts when we learn that sanctification is God doing the work for us. That's grace. If you try to do good in your own power, you will always fail.

Next, let's look at the difference between justification and sanctification regarding our righteousness. Justification is being "made right in Heaven." The moment I trusted Christ as Savior, my name was written down in Heaven as His child. Although I am not there yet, my future destiny is completely assured.

Sometimes people say they are sinners saved by grace. I know what they mean, but that's really not correct according to God's Word. I was a sinner, and I have been saved by grace. But what I am right now is a saint saved by the grace of God. When God looks at me, He sees me through the blood of His Son. To Him, I am perfect. I have been made right in God's eyes.

But I still sin. How can I be perfect in God's eyes and still sin? That's because the body of sin—what people sometimes call the sin nature—still dwells within me. It remains a strong negotiator for the things of the world until I develop my relationship with God through sanctification. Sanctification makes me "more right on earth."

The benefits of sanctification come as my developing relationship with Christ strengthens me to yield to His Spirit. Only then will I live righteously and godly in this present world. (Titus 2:12) Sanctification allows me to live the Christian life here on earth, through the power of God. Again, let me remind you that *both* justification and sanctification are works of God through grace, not works you do yourself.

Finally, let's look at the difference between justification and sanctification as it relates to knowledge. Justification means that God knows you. I often hear people say, "You need to know God so that you can go to Heaven when you die." No one goes to Heaven because they know God. You only go to Heaven when, through your faith in the shed blood of Jesus, God knows you.

Jesus said, "Many will say to me in that day, Lord, Lord, have we not prophesied in thy name? and in thy name have cast out devils? and in thy name done many wonderful works? And then will I profess unto them, *I never knew you:* depart from me, ye that work iniquity." (Matt. 7:22&23, emphasis added) Going to church and doing good works and knowing about God will not get you into Heaven. God needs to know you.

Sanctification, on the other hand is us knowing God. Peter said, "But grow in grace, and in the knowledge of our Lord and Saviour Jesus Christ." (II Pet. 3:18) As we develop a deeper understanding of who God is and our personal relationship with Him grows, we live a more victorious life.

Justification is dependent on accepted information—that Christ was crucified to pay for your sins. Sanctification is the process of developing a personal relationship with Him. Many times people use the phrase "walk with God" and it almost becomes a cliché. But that is a very accurate description of the process of sanctification. Walking is simply defined as repeated steps. As you take repeated steps under the leading and influence of the Holy Spirit, you draw closer to God and become more like Jesus. When the Holy Spirit is guiding your life and you are successfully yielding to that guidance, you will enjoy the blessings of sanctification.

To sum up, justification is best pictured by the empty cross. Jesus once and for all paid the penalty for our sins at Calvary. Sanctification is best pictured by the empty tomb. Jesus did not stay dead. The victorious life is available to us because He rose again. Paul said, "That I may know him, and the power of his resurrection." (Phil. 3:10) The power to *know Him* is found in the **resurrection**, not the **crucifixion**! Knowing Jesus—a growing personal relationship with Him—is what gives you access to that power.

BUILDING A PERSONAL RELATIONSHIP

One of the most familiar passages in the Bible is Romans 12:1 and 2. Often preachers will use these verses in talking about surrender, Christian service, and Christian living. But in these verses, Paul is really teaching us about yielding to sanctification. In fact, he is begging us to yield ourselves to God!

"I beseech you therefore, brethren, by the mercies of God, that ye present your bodies a living sacrifice, holy, acceptable unto God, which is your reasonable service. And be not conformed to this world: but be ye transformed by the renewing of your mind, that ye may prove what is that good, and acceptable, and perfect, will of God."—Romans 12:1-2

A Personal Relationship Requires Presentation

The word beseech literally means "to beg." Paul is begging us to give up our bodies to God—to present them to Him. Why is that important? It's important because sin dwells in the body. As we already saw, the sin in your body will try to negotiate with your soul to wrest control away from your spirit.

God wants us to forsake what we want to do, to be and to have in exchange for what He wants us to do, to be and to have. As Paul noted, this is a reasonable request. Paul is begging us to make the sacrifice of leading a Holy Spirit-led lifestyle. If you do not make this presentation, you will never experience the benefits of a personal relationship with

God. It's important to understand that such a presentation does not produce a personal relationship; it is merely opens the door to developing that relationship. There are further sacrifices that must also be made.

Paul next takes up the subject of conforming and transforming. He said, "And be not conformed to this world: but be ye transformed by the renewing of your mind." The crux of this verse is that we are to stop <u>thinking</u> and <u>acting</u> the way we have been, and began <u>thinking</u> and <u>acting</u> in a new way.

We cannot live the way God wants us to live—unconformed to the world but rather transformed from the world—apart from an intimate relationship with Him. Otherwise our spirit will not have enough power to defeat our body for control of our soul. So how can we change the way we think and live?

The answer is found in the conjunction *but* that connects the two phrases. I've already referenced the Schoolhouse Rock programs that used to interrupt my Saturday morning cartoons. If you ever heard the tune to Conjunction Junction, you'll never be able to get it out of your memory!

Conjunction Junction, what's your function?
Picking up words and phrases and clauses!
Conjunction Junction, how's that function?
I've got *and*, *but*, and *or*, and they get me pretty far!

Of course you remember that a conjunction puts two phrases together and makes them run right. In this case, the conjunction *but* shows us that the second phrase must precede the first phrase. Paul is teaching us that, in order to change the way we act, we must first change the way we think.

A Proper Presentation Leads to Transformation

The word transformation comes from the word metamorphosis. A metamorphosis means a change in form. The transformation, or change in form in our lives, begins with renewing the mind. Paul used the word renewing, which means to make new after destruction or depravity. That is a very accurate description of our minds after the fall.

As we saw, the first outside pressure Eve encountered was the lust of the flesh, which attacks the mind. The decay of her mind began before she reached out and took the fruit. She began to question the validity of God's words, and the allure of the fruit and the knowledge it offered outweighed obedience in her mind. Sin must gain permission from the soul before it can engage the body. Its point of entry and persuasion begins in the mind.

In the same way, the transforming of our behavior must also begin in the mind. Perhaps one of the best illustrations is the contrast between two superheroes who were popular when I was young. It was a great visual reminder of how we act and react when faced with adversity. Every week, the first television program began something like this:

"David Bruce Banner: doctor, physician. He was searching for hidden strengths that all humans have, when an accidental overdose of gamma radiation altered his body chemistry. Now, whenever David Banner becomes angry or outraged, a startling metamorphosis occurs."

Then you would see a picture of David Banner trying to change a flat tire in the pouring rain. As he tries to get the tire off, the tire iron slips and he bangs his knuckles. Suddenly, his eyes change color, his skin turns green, and he transforms into the raging creature known as the Incredible Hulk. Faced with adversity, he lacked the ability to control his reactions. That is the plight of the

SIN MUST GAIN PERMISSION FROM THE SOUL BEFORE IT CAN ENGAGE THE BODY. ITS POINT OF ENTRY AND PERSUASION BEGINS IN THE MIND.

depraved mind of man. It is so controlled by outside influences that it can change the nicest person into a snarling monster.

There was another superhero who dates back a little further who was very different. Like David Banner, he was calm and mild-mannered on the outside. But Clark Kent never changed his demeanor. No matter how hard things got or how difficult the circumstances he faced were, Clark was always calm, cool, and collected.

If a jet plane was spinning out of control toward the *Daily Planet* where Clark worked, he would just slip into a closet, pull off his suit, and fly off as Superman. He would bring the plane under control and return it and all the passengers safely to the ground. Why could Clark Kent remain calm in any situation? Because he knew that he had a hidden power within that began with a capital "S".

Our minds can be repaired so that instead of becoming monsters under outside pressure and influence, we respond in great strength through the inward persuasion of another power that begins with a capital "S"—the Holy Spirit.

The only way to repair or renew the mind is to undo what destroyed it in the first place. Adam fell when he made the choice to acquire information over developing a personal relation. We wanted to be like God in our own power. To renew our minds, we must reject focusing on the acquisition of information about God and focus on building our personal relation with God.

A Proper Transformation Leads to Conformation

Paul told us to "be not conformed to this world." The word conformed means to be poured into a mold. The things of the world's mold are shaped by the lust of the flesh, the lust of the eyes, and the pride of life. Never forget that the devil is attempting to use outside pressures to mold your behavior to his purposes. God works from the inside out and the devil works from the outside in!

Renewing your mind—abandoning, moment by moment, a focus on information for a focus on a personal relation—strengthens your inner man. As you develop the habit of communication between the Holy Spirit and your spirit, you learn to function as a Spirit-led trichotomy.

Only then can Christ live His life through you and clearly express His desires to you. As this process develops, you will be un-conformed from the world and conformed to the image of Jesus Christ. This is God's purpose and plan for your life. Paul wrote, "For whom he did foreknow, he also did predestinate to be conformed to the image of his Son, that he might be the firstborn among many brethren." (Rom. 8:29) That is to say that as a result of your conformity to the image of God, you will become a conduit of reproduction!

The stronger your personal relationship with Jesus, the more in control of your life He will be. The more in control of your life He is, the more your behavior will be in His image and likeness. The more you are molded after Jesus, the less attractive the mold of the world will become to you.

Reject what you want to do, and replace it with what Christ wants you to do. Reject what you want to have, and replace it with what Christ wants you to have. Reject what you want to be, and replace it with what Christ wants you to be. Allow Jesus Christ to duplicate His life through you as you mold and conform your behavior to Him in the power of His Spirit. That is the crucified Christian life.

A Proper Conformation Produces Documentation

Paul concludes with the result of the renewal process—"that ye may prove what is that good, and acceptable, and perfect, will of God." The word prove means to document, or to produce evidence to support. When you have presented your body to God as a living sacrifice, He begins His work in you.

As your mind is repaired, He begins to communicate to you. Your life becomes holy and acceptable to God. As your inner man is strengthened you have God's power available to un-conform from the world. He then begins to live His life through you. This brings your life into the will of God. I have experienced this process first hand in my own life. Although I do not always yield to the Spirit's power, that power is always available to me. When I do yield, my life produces evidence that I am pleasing God by fulfilling His will.

That evidence is proof or documentation of my personal relationship with God. It shows that I know what God's will is, and that I am walking after it. The more my relationship with God grows, the more I realize that it is God who is working in me to will and do of His good pleasure. (Phil. 2:13)

Of course God's plan for restoring our daily walk with Him will not unfold in our lives without resistance from the prince of this world. God's original plan for man was derailed in the Garden of Eden when Adam and Eve traded His plan for Satan's. In the same way, the devil will come and tempt you to try hard to change your own behavior rather than following God's plan to exchange your behavior. I call this the devil's plan for mismanagement.

chapter nine

THE DEVIL'S PLAN FOR MISMANAGEMENT

WHEN CHRIST RETURNED TO HEAVEN AFTER HIS RESURRECTION, THE HOLY SPIRIT CAME INTO THE LIVES OF GOD'S CHILDREN WITH POWER FROM ON HIGH. The Messiah had come just as God had promised, and through His death and resurrection the penalty for sin had been paid and the power of sin had been broken. The veil that separated the holy of holies from the people was torn apart, symbolizing that man could once again enjoy a dynamic, personal love relationship with the Creator.

Of course the devil didn't just give up because of that defeat. He still wants to control God's creation. He lost the power he had gained when man's spirit died because of sin now that Jesus had brought the birth of our new spirit. In order to regain his control, the devil needed to gain power over the internal decision making process within God's new creation.

How would he be able to do that? Would he need some new and elaborate plan to tempt man? No. He went back to the very same plan that worked against Adam and Eve in the Garden of Eden. He offers the children of God today the same system of mismanagement that he tempted Adam and Eve with—an acquisition of information about God rather than a personal relation with God.

Of course Satan has control of the lost world. His darkness tries to keep them blind to the light of the Gospel. (II Cor. 4:4) Once people are saved and become God's children, he loses his dominion over them. He cannot remain when the Holy Spirit of God comes in to live in the new believer. The light casts out darkness, no matter how great the darkness is.

So what does the devil do to regain his control? Once again he tries to deceive man through outside pressure to reject Spirit control for soul control. But in his subtlety, he offers man "good" soul control. To understand how this temptation works, we need to review what happens when a person becomes a Christian.

At the moment of salvation, our spirit comes alive and the Holy Spirit comes to live within the new believer. The power of sin over the redeemed soul is destroyed. The lure and allure of sin is minimized. As the believer offers himself a sacrifice that is alive, his mind is transformed from gathering information to building a personal relation. This transformation conforms him to the image of Christ.

As he makes the choice to serve God rather than to serve sin, he submits to the Holy Spirit and becomes more like Jesus. This is the crucified Christian life. Paul said, "For to me to live is Christ, and to die is gain." (Phil. 1:21) However the devil wants you to have a different kind of relationship with God.

His goal is to influence you through outside pressures to overlook the importance of the transformation process to your conformation into Christ's image. His plan looks good, and in fact, it will seem to be leading you right at first. But in the end, the lack of an intimate, personal relation with Jesus Christ will doom you to failure.

Here's an illustration of how this process usually fails. A lost man believes the "information" of the cross and accepts Christ as Savior. His justification is settled forever at that moment. He is sanctified, but the benefits of sanctification have not yet been experienced. The devil comes and tempts the young believer away from building an intimate, personal relationship with Christ into acquiring all the information he can about Christ..

This young believer will turn to the pastor and say, "What are the rules? What are the rules for my life, my wife, and my kids? How am I supposed to act? What can I say and when should it be said? How do I dress? How do my kids dress? How do I wear my hair? How should I spend my time? How should I spend my money? Can I go to movies? Well then, can I at least rent videos?" The list goes on and on.

The new believer is falling into the devil's trap. Rather than conforming by transforming, he is conforming by performing. The problem is that a performing will never lead to consistent behavioral modification. God never intended the Old Testament law to be a performance standard, but that's exactly what the Pharisees turned it into.

They surrounded the law with so many traditions and additional rules that they made it something very different from what it was meant to be. In fact, Jesus said they were, "Making the word of God of none effect through [their] tradition." (Mark 7:13) Just as God did not intend for man to perform under the Law before Christ's death, He does intend for man to perform to please Him under Grace either!

Performing (rather than transforming) only pleases the spectators. If you are doing the work of the Lord in your own power, He's not watching you. You've turned your back on Him in order to face the people you're trying to please or impress. Jesus said, "Take heed that ye do not your alms before men, to be seen of them: otherwise ye have no reward of your Father which is in heaven." (Matt. 6:1)

When someone is performing for those who are watching, eventually people stop watching, and eventually they stop performing. The truth is that if you are performing for the approval and applause of men, the devil has already gained control over your life. What makes this especially dangerous is that the devil will use fellow Christians as the spectators who will place outside pressure on you. They want you to control your behavior, and do not believe you can without their help. So they try to control it with a set of rules, steps and boundaries that bring about good, but dead, works!

PERFORMING (RATHER THAN TRANSFORMING) ONLY PLEASES THE SPECTATORS. IF YOU ARE DOING THE WORK OF THE LORD IN YOUR OWN POWER, HE'S NOT WATCHING YOU.

This does not mean that it is wrong to follow a set of rules. But if you are following those rules to obtain a level of righteousness, you are falling into the devil's trap. You cannot conform when you perform. Yet a personal relation with God will conform you into the image of God! This is real behavior modification. It never comes from conforming by performing.

The search for information about God must always be secondary to developing your personal relation with God. Conforming by first transforming produces a strong relationship between your spirit and the Spirit of God. Conforming by performing produces frustration, confusion, and ultimately, failure.

Being transformed produces a level of righteous living that following a set of rules will never be able to develop. Righteous living as a byproduct of a personal relationship with God produces Christian joy. The Psalmist said, "Thou wilt shew me the path of life:

in thy presence is fulness of joy; at thy right hand there are pleasures for evermore." (Psalm 16:11)

The Christian life is supposed to be filled with joy, not with drudgery. Yet too many believers struggle without the joy of the Lord. Why? Because they have fallen into the devil's snare of trying to perform to gain acceptance. Let's look at the difference between conforming by transforming and conforming by performing step by step.

Conforming by Transforming – Yielding to Internal Influence

1. The Holy Spirit of God communicates to the spirit of man what He thinks, feels, and wants us to do in a particular circumstance. This takes place in the inner man, where the Spirit dwells with your spirit.
2. The spirit of man processes that truth and communicates it clearly to the soul.
3. The devil counters God's plan with an external influence (usually with something good but not what God has in mind, or with something bad). I call this a circumstance of life—a "whammy."
4. That outside influence causes the body of man, to negotiate with the soul to reject the spirit's leading and give in to sinful wishes. Remember that the body has to negotiate because sin no longer has power over a believer's soul. The redeemed soul must then choose, just as Adam and Eve did, between something that will strengthen his walk with God or hinder it.
5. As the inner man is strengthened through a personal relation with God, the soul will by faith reject the body and yield his members as instruments of righteousness. This happens when he dies to his body's desires (a daily process) and yields to the

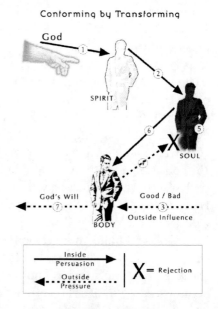

life of Christ. Christ's life can then be lived and expressed through our life.

6. Since the soul has submitted to the spirit, it commands the body to do as God leads. The body then steps forward on the right path. By faith, the believer is "walking after the spirit" and not fulfilling the lusts of the flesh. (Gal. 5:16)

7. Thus the believer is living according to the will of God.

This is Christian Living 101. A believer living this way is enjoying Christian liberty in his life, and as a by-product of that is enjoying the fruits of a dynamic Christian life. A believer living in this way does great damage to the devil's domain. That's the way God intends for us to live. But what happens when we follow the devil's system?

Conforming by Performing – Yielding to Outside Influences

1. As believers, we face circumstances in life (whammies) that require us to make choices. We need a leading from God to determine our direction. This leading comes from the internal influence of the Holy Spirit found in our inner man.

2. If we are patient and open to the Lord's leading, we will receive that direction. Our spirit then communicates that guidance from God to our soul.

3. The devil tries to influence us away from God's leading through outside pressure. Remember that with a child of God, the devil usually will not tempt you with a bad influence. He is more likely to try to offer you an option that is good, yet contrary to the leading of the Holy Spirit. The Bible says Satan is transformed into an angel of light. (II Cor. 11:14) He tries to give direction in such a way as to deceive us into thinking it comes from God and will result in good. He offers us a different good to replace God's good.

4. The body transmits this good yet fleshly alternative to the soul. The soul is faced with a choice between two things that each seems good. However, one of those choices will strengthen the relationship with God while the other will weaken it. Only the choice that comes from God will build your relationship with Him. The other, even though it is apparently good, comes from an evil spirit.

5. The soul of a performer has knowledge of God, perhaps even a lot of knowledge. However because he has focused on performing for

others, his personal relation with God as been non-conforming. This hinders the "still, small voice" because his spiritual intuition is low.

6. Since he considers good works to be what makes him righteous, he is prone to reject the Spirit's leading for the opportunity to perform good works in his own power.

7. The soul submits to the body and rejects what has been revealed as God's will for good will. Good will is doing good things man's way rather than God's.

Conforming by Performing

A perfect example of this truth would be a woman who is convicted by the Spirit that she should be involved in the church's soul winning program. God is clearly leading her, and she is being challenged and is under conviction. Satan notices this and offers her a good alternative to becoming a soul winner.

He points out through an external influence—maybe something as harmless as the church bulletin or the suggestion of a friend—that the church needs good singers for the choir. Knowing that God has blessed her with a good voice, she must weigh her leadings. She must choose between God's good leading and an alternative good leading.

She is being led by God to go soul winning. This fulfills a command of Scripture and pleases God. She is being pulled to sing in the choir. This fulfills a need in the church and pleases people. She chooses to join the choir, not in addition to soul winning, but in place of it. She has submitted to the external influences of alternative opportunities.

For the next thirty years, that woman will sing in the church choir. Never again will she feel so strongly compelled to win souls. Why? Because when she stood at a crossroads of life, she submitted to the wrong influence. Her performance in the choir substitutes for obedience to God's leading.

Please don't misunderstand this illustration. Singing in the choir is an opportunity to minister. If God leads you to join the choir, you should do so immediately. But singing in the choir cannot substitute for something different that the Holy Spirit is leading you to do. The woman in our illustration will perform week after week in front of the church, but it will never help her conform to the image of Christ!

Singing in the choir will never give her the joy and liberty that following God's will would have done. She will never be fully content. She is living after the flesh instead of in the spirit. She is doing good. But flesh is flesh. If we are walking after the flesh, we cannot please God, no matter how much good we do!

Most Christians do not even realize how this process affects their lives. They either do not know or forget that the devil does not mind if they do good, as long as they do it in their own strength. They mistakenly believe that performing can substitute transforming.

The devil does not mind at all if you do good, as long as it is not in obedience to the Spirit of God. A submissive believer who is enjoying a dynamic love relationship with Jesus Christ will experience the abundant Christian life. That deep relationship with the Creator brings a level of contentment that nothing else can provide. That's because the fruit (or outcome) of the Spirit is joy!

When we are being transformed—that is when we are using information merely as fuel to build our personal relationship with God—the result is our conformation. Through yielding to the inner man, the presence, leading and conviction of the Holy Spirit is heard and heeded. The conviction, challenges and comfort He brings becomes a strong force in our lives. Submission to Him brings a rewarding relationship with God. This is the abundant Christian life.

THE DEVIL DOES NOT MIND AT ALL IF YOU DO GOOD, AS LONG AS IT IS NOT IN OBEDIENCE TO THE SPIRIT OF GOD.

When we are focused on performing—that is when we are trying to modify our behavior based on a set of rules, steps, or boundaries that are enforced by external influences—the result is emptiness. The presence, leading and conviction of the Holy Spirit is weak and is not followed. Trying to act like God in your own power is an incredibly frustrating way to live. This is not the abundant Christian life; instead it is what I call the redundant Christian life.

So if many Christians cannot discern whether they are performing or transforming, how can we tell which we are doing? The easiest way is to determine how we respond to the "whammies" of life. If we follow internal persuasion, then we are developing our inner man through transformation.

If you have never experienced a strong personal relationship with God, you may not know what you are missing. You may be unsure how the transformed Christian life feels. Some people object to this and say that the Christian life isn't supposed to be a feeling. But isn't joy a feeling? Can you feel it when you are expressing love? Doesn't peace feel good? How about goodness and gentleness? Don't they bring a good feeling into your heart.

While it is true that feelings should not rule our lives, you do feel good when you are right with God. Take it from a former alcoholic—temperance feels REALLY GOOD! All of these things are fruits of the Spirit—that is they are a natural result of yielding to His control.

To understand the difference between conforming by performing and conforming by transforming on a practical level, we need to understand the fundamental difference between "how God acts," "how man acts," and "how man acts when he is trying to act like God."

When we understand how God acts during "whammies" we will see how we are supposed to act while transforming. Likewise, when we see how we act when we are acting like God, we will be able to determine when we are performing. And that will be the subject of our next section.

TALL LAW

When Man Tries To Act Like God

INTRODUCTION

MUCH OF THE MATERIAL IN THIS SECTION COVERS THE SAME TOPIC THAT WE ADDRESSED IN CHAPTER NINE OF THE REFORMERS UNANIMOUS ADDICTIONS PROGRAM TEXTBOOK, *NEVERTHELESS I LIVE.* Here we're going to look at the ways we act and react to the various circumstances of life.

This section was designed by Reformers Unanimous International to be a 12-20 week discipleship course for churched members. The purpose is to explain the difference between the redundant Christian life and the abundant Christian life. Before we begin this study, however, I want to stop and give you a brief explanation of two key Bible phrases taught in this section—"in the spirit" and "after the flesh"—that are crucial to your understanding of what we're going to learn.

Please be willing to spend the time to study and thoroughly understand each of these lessons. Some of the things we'll see may be hard to grasp at first. But as you read, ask God to help you understand these truths and give you grace to apply them to your life. By doing so, you will find a freedom that many Christians never experience, even after years of learning and living for God.

In the first section, we discussed the role God intends for the inner man to play in our lives. God is looking to live through us in order to produce His power in our lives so that we can do great exploits for Him. If God is going to continually live His life in us, we must remain submissive to Him. Therefore, as we begin to develop spiritually, we ought to be able to determine through personal behavioral observation when He is leading us and when we are instead leading ourselves.

As we have explained, when the outer man is in submission to the desires of our body, we are "walking after the flesh." Even if we are doing good things, if we are doing them in our own strength, we are still "walking after the flesh." That's because we are doing good in our own power rather than in God's power.

In Galatians 2:21, Paul told the church of Galatia that this type of behavior frustrates the grace of God. Grace is when God is doing the work. To frustrate in this context means to interrupt. What Paul is saying is that these Christians were actually interrupting what God was trying to do for them.

Look at how Paul said they were interrupting God's work. "Are ye so foolish? Having begun in the Spirit, are ye now made perfect by the flesh?" (Gal. 3:3) These Christians had been saved—justified by the Spirit of God. That's what "having begun in the Spirit" refers to. The problem was that, rather than following God's plan for them to enjoy their sanctification, they were trying to do it themselves in their own power.

They had ceased to submit to the Spirit's work and were trying to develop spiritually in their own power. This is an incredibly frustrating way to live. If frustrates us, because even if we are doing good, there is emptiness in place of joy. It frustrates God, because it does not allow Him to perform the good work in our lives that He wants to perform. Living under soul control instead of Spirit control is frustrating all the way around.

> "This I say then, Walk in the Spirit, and ye shall not fulfil the lust of the flesh. For the flesh lusteth against the Spirit, and the Spirit against the flesh; and these are contrary the one to the other; so that ye cannot do the things that ye would. But if ye be led of the Spirit, ye are not under the law. Now the works of the flesh are manifest, which are these; Adultery, fornication, uncleanness, lasciviousness, Idolatry, witchcraft, hatred, variance, emulations, wrath, strife, seditions, heresies, Envyings, murders, drunkenness, revellings, and such like: of the which I tell you before, as I have also told you in time past, that they which do such things shall not inherit the kingdom of God. But the fruit of the Spirit is love, joy, peace, longsuffering, gentleness, goodness, faith, Meekness, temperance: against such there is no law." —Galatians 5:16-23

This passage clearly explains the battle between our flesh and the Spirit of God. Paul starts by saying "For the flesh lusteth against the Spirit, and the Spirit against the flesh." This simply tells us that our body is in conflict with the Spirit for control of our souls. Both our body and the Spirit long to lead the soul of man.

Then we read, "and these are contrary the one to the other." It's very obvious that the desires of the body and the desires of the Spirit are opposite. There is no middle ground. You will either be lead by the Spirit as your soul submits to Him, or you will be ruled by the body as you rebel against the Spirit's leading. Even if you are doing good, it's nothing more than self-control.

YOU WILL EITHER BE LEAD BY THE SPIRIT AS YOUR SOUL SUBMITS TO HIM, OR YOU WILL BE RULED BY THE BODY AS YOU REBEL AGAINST THE SPIRIT'S LEADING.

Most people think self-control is a good thing, but it's not. While it is better than no control, the only option that is obedient to God is Spirit control. Romans 7:18 says, "in me (that is, in my flesh) dwelleth no good thing."

The last phrase of verse 17 identifies and explains the greatest struggle in the Christian life when it says, "ye cannot do the things that ye would." We want to do the right things and we try to do the right things, but we fail. The problem is that **we** are trying to do them. Paul tells us this effort is doomed—ye cannot do the things that ye would. It is impossible.

Maybe you've never realized this truth before. But you *cannot* live the Christian life in your own power. No matter how hard you try to do better, only Christ can live the Christian life! You have to stop trying and let God do the work. That's grace! Grace is when God does the work; Law is when man does the work. If you are trying to do what you should, you will ultimately fail and lose your joy. However if you let God do what He wants you to do, victory is certain.

Most of us realize how foolish it is to try to save ourselves from our sins. We understand that justification only comes through the grace of God. Yet many sincere, well-meaning believers try to experience the benefits of sanctification by doing good works in the energy of our flesh. That never works. Just as we are saved by grace alone, we are experience our sanctification in the same way.

Paul further explains this truth in the next verse. He wrote, "But if ye be led by the Spirit, ye are not under the law." If God is leading and we are following in step, then we are walking after the Spirit. This frees us from the law, where we try to do the work. It places us in a new realm where God does the work for us. What an incredibly enjoyable place to be!

When God is in control and our soul is in submission to the Spirit, He can accomplish things through us which we can never accomplish when our flesh is in control. When our flesh is in control, there are certain actions or reactions that can be expected. We'll look later on at the "good" works of the flesh, but first Paul lists the evil works of the flesh.

Paul uses the phrase "the works of the flesh are manifest." Works means effort. The flesh is the soul under the influence and control of the body. Thus Paul's phrase means the efforts of the soul under the influence and control of the body are manifest. Manifest means "to make evident." Therefore when the body is in control, the things that we do provide evidence of that fact. Here are the bad works of the flesh:

Adultery: sex outside of marriage
Fornication: sex before marriage
Uncleanness: sexual deviance
Lasciviousness: sexual excess
Idolatry: valuing something over your relationship with God
Witchcraft: being under the influence of the devil
Hatred: having a great dislike for another
Variance: being argumentative
Emulation: an unhealthy desire for superiority
Wrath: desire to get even and have revenge
Strife: spreading angry contention
Sedition: raising commotion
Heresies: errors in the fundamental doctrines of God
Envying: general uneasiness with the happiness of others
Murders: premeditating killing of another human being
Drunkenness: to be habitually intoxicated by alcohol
Reveling: carousing in a party-like atmosphere

Now there are some things on that list that I have never done. But there are others that at one time were a real problem for me. Sometimes they still are! When they were (or are) it is evident that I am following the desires of my flesh, walking in my own strength instead of in the Spirit.

Of course we cannot live perfect and sinless lives. We will at times fail when we are tested. But if one or more of these "works of the flesh" is a consistent problem in your life and there is no conviction or chastening from God, you should question your salvation. Paul said, "They which do such things shall not inherit the kingdom of God." He is issuing a very serious warning to people who think they are children of God but live like they're children of the devil.

If this person is saved, then these fleshly behaviors are actions of a person who is rebellious to the Spirit that lives within their inner man. God is not in control of the life that produces evil works. There is an alternative, however. We are not helpless in the battle between good and evil. We can live a victorious Christian life—what I refer to as a little bit of Heaven on earth.

When Christ is living through us, we don't have to wait for Heaven to live the kind of life that we will enjoy when we get there. The transforming power of God's system of management is seen in this passage. After reciting a long list of evil deeds in I Corinthians 6:9&10, Paul acknowledges that some believers were guilty of these sins as well. He said, "Such were some of you".

Maybe you've seen the bumper sticker that says, "Christians aren't perfect; just forgiven." You may have some terrible sins in your past. But you don't have to live in the guilt and shame of that past. Look at what Paul said, "Such were some of you: but ye are washed, but ye are sanctified, but ye are justified in the name of the Lord Jesus, and by the Spirit of God." (I Cor. 6:11)

What a marvelous gift and opportunity God offers us as His children! He can wash us from the filthiness of our sins through justification and give us a Spirit-filled lifestyle through sanctification. Through faith in the Lord Jesus Christ, we are justified by His grace. Through submission to the Holy Spirit, we experience the benefits of sanctification by that same grace.

We've seen the list of evil behavior that is produced by "walking after the flesh." It's important to remember that a believer cannot walk "in the flesh." Justification has removed that possibility. However, a believer can still walk "after the flesh." When we choose to submit to the sinful desires of the body rather than the inner promptings of the Spirit, we are choosing to follow a path that produces evil works at worst and dead works at best. (For a more detailed study of the difference between walking in the flesh and walking after the flesh, please see the Reformers Challenger Workbook section on Romans 6 and 8.)

Romans chapter 8 explains the differences between walking "after" and walking "in" the flesh. It also explains what walking after the

Spirit means. I've highlighted the important phrases that show the difference. Please read this passage slowly, and take time to meditate on the words.

"There is therefore now no condemnation to them which are in Christ Jesus, who walk not after the flesh, but after the Spirit. For the law of the Spirit of life in Christ Jesus hath made me free from the law of sin and death. For what the law could not do, in that it was weak through the flesh, God sending his own Son in the likeness of sinful flesh, and for sin, condemned sin in the flesh. (Stop and reread first sentence before continuing.) That the righteousness of the law might be fulfilled in us, who walk not after the flesh, but after the Spirit. For they that are after the flesh do mind the things of the flesh; but they that are after the Spirit the things of the Spirit. So then they that are in the flesh (those who are unsaved) cannot please God. But ye are not in the flesh, but in the Spirit, if so be that the Spirit of God dwell in you. And if Christ be in you, the body is dead because of sin; but the Spirit is life because of righteousness."—Romans 8:1-5, 8-10

This passage tells us that if we are in Christ, that is if we are under His influence, we will not experience feelings of condemnation. However, It is possible for a child of God to suffer feelings of condemnation, if he is not walking after the Spirit.

However, these feelings of guilt that condemn us are not from God but from the devil. When we follow the leading of the Holy Spirit and do right, we do not suffer from feelings of guilt and unworthiness. Thus the law of the Spirit, in contrast to the old law, offers us freedom from condemnation.

The word law refers to "a rule of conduct." Thus if we yield to the rule of conduct that the Holy Spirit is prompting, we will be free from, not only the penalty of sin, but also the power of sin. That is what sanctification is all about. Walking according to His inner rule of conduct is walking "after the Spirit"—in essence, following His direction.

When we reject His leading, we are choosing to give away our freedom from the power of sin. We are instead following "after the flesh" as it leads us astray from the life God wants us to enjoy. It is vital to understand that most of the time when we fail to yield to the Holy Spirit, it is a failure of our faith in our inner leader.

Sometimes our own fear of this newfound freedom leads us to choose to remain in bondage. Sometimes we do not truly believe that God will do all that He has promised. Faith—which comes from hearing, reading and studying God's Word (Rom. 10:17) helps us overcome those doubts.

After Abraham Lincoln signed the Emancipation Proclamation, all of the slaves in the South were free. But of course their masters didn't share that information with them, so they continued to live in slavery. Even after the news of their deliverance reached them, some slaves made the choice to continue to serve their former masters. They chose to remain in bondage. That did not change the fact that legally they were free. But their lives did not change because they had rejected their freedom.

That is exactly what can happen to you as a believer after your conversion. Though God has freed you from the power of sin, you can still choose to follow after it. **Sin has no power over you except the power you choose to give it.** Through faith you can stop living under the law of sin and death and start living under the law of the Spirit of life that makes you free! Romans 8:2 says, "For the law of the Spirit of life in Christ Jesus hath made me free from the law of sin and death."

With this truth in mind, let's look back at Galatians 5 and our study of the lusts of the flesh. It is usually obvious when someone is engaging in these visible sins. They produce outward effects that are evidence of wrong choices. What Paul calls the works of the flesh are what I call "bad flesh"—we can tell by looking that these things are wrong.

However there is also another kind of flesh. It is a type of fleshly behavior that most people, even people who've been saved for years, do not recognize. In contrast to the works of the flesh Paul listed, this type of flesh does not produce visibly wicked acts. In Galatians 3:1, Paul said this flesh "bewitches" or fascinates Christians, pulling them away from the truth.

It is "good flesh"—that is, doing good things in our strength and power. I believe it is the single greatest problem facing Christianity today. The "bad flesh" is *unrighteous* behavior. The fruit of the Spirit is *righteous* behavior. But "good flesh" is neither unrighteous nor righteous. It is *self-righteous* behavior.

This is one of Satan's greatest tools. He knows that the Holy Spirit will produce strong convictions in the life of a believer who is engaging in the unrighteous works of the flesh. He may be able to entice God's children away from following the Spirit to walk after the bad flesh, but that is not a permanent solution from his viewpoint. The conviction of the Spirit and the chastening of the Lord will often lead the believer back out of this lifestyle.

So Satan needs a more subtle means of pulling God's children away from His will and keeping them there. The Bible tells us that Satan is "transformed into an angel of light." (II Cor. 11:14) He comes to offer a counterfeit spiritual direction that leads us to do good, but in our own power rather than in the power of God. The result is "good flesh" or self-righteousness.

Doing good in our own power is very appealing to our sense of pride and self worth. That's why Paul described it as fascinating, drawing our attention away and interrupting us from God's plan. The devil's plan is not primarily to tempt us into gross evil at first. Instead he offers us alternatives that look similar to what God would want. He does this to deceive us into slipping into self-righteousness.

In Galatians, Paul lists nine actions and reactions and calls them the fruit of the Spirit. (For a more detailed study of the fruit of the Spirit and the devil's counterfeits to each, see the Reformers Unanimous Strongholds Study Course or the 12-20 week discipleship course *Gaining Remaining Fruit*) "But the fruit of the Spirit is love, joy, peace, longsuffering, gentleness, goodness, faith, Meekness, temperance; against such there is no law." (Gal. 5:22&23)

DOING GOOD IN OUR OWN POWER IS VERY APPEALING TO OUR SENSE OF PRIDE AND SELF WORTH.

The word "fruit" means outcome or result. Thus, the fruit of the Spirit is the outcome or result of His leading in our lives. In every circumstance of life, the Holy Spirit will lead you in how to respond. He chooses the response that will honor and glorify Christ. You must choose whether to yield to His leading.

Realizing that God offers nine possible responses to every circumstance of life, how many responses do you think the devil will counter-offer? Of course he has nine as well. So assuming that you are going to respond in any given situation, there are eighteen alternatives— nine correct, and nine wrong. One of the weaknesses of the church today is that too many believers have a weak personal relation with God. Thus they are unable to distinguish between righteous promptings of the Spirit and self-righteous promptings of the flesh.

In Section Two, we're going to examine each of those eighteen alternative actions and reactions—the nine that are correct along with the devil's counterfeits. In this way you can observe through your own responses to adverse circumstances whether you are living righteously under the influence of the Spirit, or whether you are a "good Christian" living self-righteously under the influence of the flesh.

The nine responses of the Spirit break down into three categories, each affecting a different part of our lives. Love, joy, and peace are transforming—they change our inner being. Longsuffering, gentleness, and goodness are conforming—they change our outer being. Faith, meekness and temperance are reforming—they affect our new being.

LOVE VS. SELF-LOVE

GOD KNOWS THAT A PERSON WILL NEVER MODIFY HIS BEHAVIOR UNTIL HE FIRST CHANGES HIS THINKING. So His responses, produced when we follow the Spirit's leading, begin by first transforming us on the inside. If you do not have love, joy or peace in your heart, it can go undetected for a long time. These are inner responses. God wants these three fruits to be our inner man's response when we face adversity. When our soul yields to His Spirit, we will respond properly.

God Offers the Fruit of the Spirit—Love

In English, we use one word for love. A person may say he loves his wife, and that he loves ice cream. But in Greek, there are several different words for love. The Greek word *eros*, taken from the name of their god of love, describes a physical love. (This word is not used in the New Testament.)

The Greek word *philos* refers to an affection or fondness. The City of Brotherly Love—Philadelphia—takes its name from this word. It is talking about a love between friends. The Bible also uses a form of this word, *philostorgos* to describe the love parents have for their children.

The highest form of love is described by the word *agape*. This kind of love is "the willing, sacrificial giving of oneself for the benefit of others without thought of return." This is the kind of love God has for us. It is this word that is used to describe the love that is produced by following the Holy Spirit.

What did God do to demonstrate His love toward us? "For God so loved the world that he gave his only begotten Son, that whosoever believeth in him should not perish, but have everlasting life." (John 3:16) He willingly gave of Himself for our benefit without any thought of return. That is the greatest gift of all!

God the Father was not alone in His demonstration of love. Jesus, His Son, willingly came to earth as a sacrifice for our sins. Following the leading of the Spirit, His response of love led him to lay down His life for us. In Ephesians 5:2, Paul encourages us to follow His example. "And walk in love, as Christ also hath loved us, and hath given himself for us an offering and a sacrifice to God..."

In fact if we do not yield to the same spirit in order to demonstrate love toward others, the world will never be convinced that we are followers of Jesus Christ. He said, "A new commandment give I unto you, That ye love one another; as I have loved you, that ye also love one another. By this shall all men know that ye are my disciples, if ye have love one to another." (John 11:34-35)

This command to love others is repeated throughout the Bible. First John 3:23 says, "And this is his commandment, That we should believe on the name of his Son Jesus Christ, and love one another, as he gave us commandment." Matthew 22:37-40 says, "Jesus said unto him, Thou shalt love the Lord thy God with all thy heart , and with all thy soul, and with all thy mind. This is the first and great commandment. And the second is like unto it, Thou shalt love thy neighbor as thyself. On these two commandments hang all the law and the prophets."

God is asking us to willingly and sacrificially give of ourselves for the benefit of others. Love is God's tool for showing unselfish favor to undeserving people. We can do many things for undeserving people and make great sacrifices for them. Yet if those acts are not done under the influence of the Spirit in true love, they will not bring a positive result.

We see this truth taught in I Corinthians 13. Paul said, "Though I speak with the tongues of men and of angels, and have not charity, I am become as sounding brass, or a tinkling cymbal. And though I have the gift of prophecy, and understand all mysteries, and all knowledge; and though I have all faith, so that I could remove mountains, and have not charity, I am nothing. And though I bestow all my goods to feed the poor, and though I give my body to be burned, and have not charity, it profiteth me nothing."

Look at the good things Paul describes—eloquent speech in many languages, great understanding of the truths of God, mighty faith that is able to move mountains, giving away everything that you possess, and dying as a martyr. Those are very impressive things. Yet without Spirit-led charity—love, they are nothing. All of the fleshy-led sacrifices we could ever make have no value at all.

Let's look at the qualities of Spirit-led love. "Charity suffereth long, and is kind; charity envieth not; charity vaunteth not itself, is not puffed up, Doth not behave itself unseemly, seeketh not her own, is not easily provoked, thinketh no evil; Rejoiceth not in iniquity, but rejoiceth in truth; Beareth all thing, believeth all things, hopeth all things, endureth all things. Charity never faileth;" (I Cor. 13:4-8) Let me dissect and define these verses a little further.

Suffereth long and is kind: puts up with inconveniences
Envieth not: lifts up others rather than self
Vaunteth not itself: is not proud or stuck up
Doth not behave itself unseemly: does what is right
Seeketh not her own: looks for ways to help others
Is not easily provoked: responds properly
Thinketh no evil: thinks correctly
Rejoiceth not in iniquity: doesn't enjoy what is not right
Rejoiceth in truth: does get excited about what is right
Beareth all things: carries the weight
Believeth all things: gives the benefit of the doubt
Hopeth all things: always hopes for the best
Endureth all things: keeps on keeping on
Never faileth: works every time!

If we were honest, we'd have to admit that our service to others does not always manifest itself in these actions and reactions. Sometimes we do achieve this level. But other times we behave in a somewhat selfish manner as we try to do good things in our own power and are fleshly-led. Why does that happen?

We may fail because we do not recognize that the devil has a counterfeit version of the love that is a fruit of the Spirit. Notice how subtle he is. He will not tempt us with the work of the flesh—hatred—that is the opposite of love. We would easily recognize that as being wrong. So Satan stimulates and tempts us, not to hatred, but to a self-righteous response when we do our good deeds for others. He wants us to show love in our own power, not God's. This kind of love is not God's kind of love. I call it self-love.

We Often Prefer the Work of the Flesh—Self-Love

We said that the love that is produced by yielding to the Spirit is a love that unselfishly gives for the benefit of others without thought of return. The fleshly alternative of self-love may give just as much or even more than the Spirit-led love, but it is a giving that is done with selfish expectations of return on the part of the giver.

Do you know someone in your church who serves God, sacrificially investing a great deal of time and energy? However if the pastor fails to thank him at least periodically from the pulpit, he gets offended and quits. If he is not at least occasionally receiving praise and attention for his service, he is not motivated, and may stop serving all together. A man like that is not really serving God; he is serving self. He is doing good works in the energy of the flesh. The true test of a servant is if a man acts like one when he is being treated like one!

THE TRUE TEST OF A SERVANT IS IF A MAN ACTS LIKE ONE WHEN HE IS BEING TREATED LIKE ONE!

I once had a student in Reformers Unanimous who slipped in his recovery and engaged in drug use. When he came to me, he seemed genuinely sorry and repentant for what he had done. As I counseled him, I asked him to tell me the events that led to his relapse. He said it was because he did not believe that his wife loved him.

I found that hard to believe. While he was on his drug binge, she had demonstrated her love toward him in many ways. She had even come to my office seeking counsel on how to help him. So I asked him, "What makes you think your wife does not love you?" He replied, "I work hard all week long at my job to provide a good living for my family. All I ask for is a hot meal and some clean clothes. I come home tired and have to eat something she just threw together or picked up at a drive thru. She never does the laundry, and the house is always a mess!"

Well, that might have sounded convincing, but I knew a few facts about the situation that he left out! His wife worked a full time job as a nurse, often working up to sixty hours per week. And she was taking care of three children who were under eight. To top it off, because he was working so hard, he paid a neighbor boy to take care of the lawn (from his wife's wages!) but wouldn't let her get help with the housework. I don't know, but I've been told that men can be pigs!

Now ladies, please stop reading that last paragraph to your

husbands; I'm not talking about him! Suffice it to say that he had a very unrealistic definition and expectation when it came to love. The truth is that both of them misunderstood what the other's real problem in the relationship was.

The wife believed that her husband's problem was his drug addiction. He believed her problem was that she did not love him. Both conclusions were wrong. The biggest problem that man had was that he did not love his wife—at least not the way God wanted him to love her. He did give, sometimes sacrificially, for her benefit, but he had selfish motives. He wanted and expected something in return.

That sounds fair to us, which is a good example of how deceitful Satan is. Self-love always demands a return for what it gives. Godly love demands nothing in return. This man is a Christian, but in this instance he was not living as a good one. If you asked most people, they would say he was not being a good Christian because he was doing drugs. But his real problem was that he was not yielding to the Spirit of love.

By yielding to the Spirit, he would exhibit the fruit of love, true and godly love, that would prompt him to give to his wife unselfishly. In return, she would most likely reciprocate with biblical love. Even if she did not, another fruit of the Spirit (longsuffering) would keep him from becoming discouraged and reverting to his old habit of drug use.

It was not a mere suggestion when Jesus said, "This is my commandment, That ye love one another, as I have loved you. Greater love hath no man than this, that a man lay down his life for his friends." (John 15:12-13)

chapter two

JOY VS. FRUSTRATION

JOY IS ONE OF THE MOST ENJOYABLE FRUITS OF THE SPIRIT TO EXPERIENCE IN YOUR DAILY LIFE, BUT AT THE SAME TIME IT IS ONE OF THE MOST DIFFICULT IN WHICH TO YIELD. Understand this: we lack joy only because we fail to yield to it! Most Christians think joy is missing in their lives because of something they do not have. The truth is we are full of the joy of the Lord; we just fail to yield to the Holy Spirit, so rather than it being our strength, it becomes our weakness.

Joy is defined as a "cheerful, calm delight in all the circumstances of life." Now we've already seen that God will place us in situations that will try our faith. Those situations and circumstances are designed to break the outer man (our soul) and develop the inner man (our spirit). As the inner man grows and develops, we become more of a Spirit-led believer when we yield to His prompting.

Living a Christ-like life under the power of the Holy Spirit is the best way for us to influence the lives of others. This maximizes our God-given gifts for the benefit of our families, our churches, our communities, and His Kingdom. This is the life of Christ flowing through us.

This process is described in Romans 8:28-29.

"And we know that all things work together for good to them that love God, to them who are the called according to his purpose. For whom he did foreknow, he also did predestinate to be conformed to the image of his Son, that he might be the firstborn among many brethren." -Romans 8:28-29

Let's dissect and define these verses phrase by phrase.

All things: everything that happens, both good and bad
work together: produce a result
for good: in a way that is advantageous
love God: willingly give oneself without thought of return
His purpose: to be conformed to the image of Christ
foreknow: know in advance
predestinate: pre-plan or ordain beforehand
conformed: poured into a mold
image of His Son: the likeness of Christ
firstborn: first in order of birth
many brethren: others become brothers as a result

God Offers the Fruit of the Spirit—Joy

Understanding God's purpose in allowing various circumstances to come in our lives sheds a new light on our trials, adversity, hardship and persecution. Everything that happens to us, both good and bad, is intended to produce a positive, Spirit-led action or reaction. Knowing this also shows us the danger of rejecting the Spirit's leading to respond to a particular circumstance with the fruit of joy.

You see, when difficult circumstances arise, we are actually being given the opportunity to express joy. We can rejoice in any circumstance because we understand God is working. Meditating on His plan reminds us that everything that happens is for our good and for His glory. This truth further reminds us that by yielding to the Spirit and displaying joy, we could be leading others closer to becoming a fellow believer in Christ.

The cheerful acceptance and calm delight in difficult circumstances produces a hole in the outer man that allows the inner man to shine through. Some difficult circumstances are long-lasting. For example, Paul never was given freedom from his thorn in the flesh. But often when we respond properly to adversity, it often removes the "edge." The difficulties often fade away or become easier to manage.

Like all of the fruits, joy has a fleshly alternative. The devil offers another counterfeit that stimulates our flesh and produces a self-righteous response. It is the work of the flesh—Frustration. This is a far cry from Spirit-led joy, yet many believers prefer the level of contentment that comes from a continually frustrated life.

We Often Prefer the Work of the Flesh—Frustration

I define frustration as a "rejection or unhappy refusal in the circumstances of life." In any unwanted circumstance, we can choose to respond either with joy or with frustration. The truth is that most of our fellow Christians will accept either response as good behavior!

Most Christians do not identify frustration as a work of the flesh. They will respect a display of joy, but they will pity a display of frustration. But frustration is not acceptable. It stems from negative thoughts, desires, and emotions. If the heart looks to the soul rather than to the spirit, we are guaranteed to respond after the flesh. That's why Proverbs 4:23 says, "Keep thy heart with all diligence, for out of it are the issues of life." You cannot respond properly to life's difficult circumstances if your heart is consumed with negative, pessimistic, critical thinking. You will automatically reject joy and yield to frustration.

Many people when counseling or talking to someone who is enduring difficult circumstances will say, "I understand your frustration." That's like saying, "I understand your crack cocaine addiction." Good flesh is just as bad as bad flesh. We cannot please God walking after the flesh, no matter how many good things we are doing. Regardless of what justification we may give, frustration is *never* an appropriate response.

Remember God's purpose for allowing adversity in your life:
>To wound the outer man
>To allow the inner man to shine through
>To display to others your love for God
>To conform you to be like Christ
>To lead others to salvation in Christ

If you respond to circumstances after the flesh, you will be forced to keep facing those same circumstances over and over again to bring about God's determined results. Furthermore, if you do not yield to joy, you may suffer even more severe circumstances.

God is going to break down our flesh and develop His Spirit in our lives. If you want to be like Christ, you can be! But you must allow God to place you into circumstances that will wound you. Then, you must properly respond to that circumstance. Only then will you be a refined vessel (Proverbs 25:4) ready to be used.

Of course this is easier said than done. Many times I have remembered this truth to late to apply it! Even if you've never heard this truth before, you can probably look back at your life and see how it applies. When you accept things (responding with joy) they usually get better. When you reject things (responding with frustration) they usually get worse.

Only yielding to the Spirit produces the fruit of joy. That joy brings Christ-likeness and the conversion of unbelievers. You have a choice between the fruit of the Spirit—Joy, and the work of the flesh—Frustration in every circumstance of life. Refusing to choose joy keeps you in bondage to the flesh, and simply produces repeated difficult circumstances.

chapter three
PEACE VS. WORRY

PEACE IS "BEING SAFE FROM HARM IN SPIRIT, MIND AND BODY." Why is peace such an important and necessary fruit in the life of a believer? Well consider this. Christians who yield to the fruit of love and joy are living under the influence of God. They live godly lives, because they are "in Christ." What does the Bible say about Christians who live godly lives in Christ Jesus?

"But thou hast fully known my doctrine, manner of life, purpose, faith, longsuffering, charity, patience, Persecutions, afflictions, which came unto me at Antioch, at Iconium, at Lystra; Yea, **and all that will live godly in Christ Jesus shall suffer persecution.**" II Timothy 3:10-12

We need peace because of persecution! Paul explained to Timothy that if he lived a godly life under the influence of the Spirit, then he could expect to suffer persecution. Persecution in the twenty-first century is one of the most misunderstood of Christian experiences. If we were to ask most godly believers if they had suffered persecution, they would say "no." Most Christians today think of persecution as being stoned to death or martyred in some other way for the cause of the Gospel. But failing to understand persecution keeps us from truly understanding the need for peace and the role it plays.

God Offers the Fruit of the Spirit—Peace

Persecution may include physical pain or even death, but the basic definition of persecution is "pursuit for the purpose of oppression." We sometimes talk about a demonic force called oppression. This is outside pressure that intends to lead us to step away from the Spirit's leading and walk after the flesh. A lot can be said about satanic oppression. I have written an entire book entitled "Why Is Everybody Crying?" It is an exposé on the destructive nature of satanic oppression.

There is no doubt that the devil will pursue godly, Spirit-led believers in an effort to oppress them and render them useless. He will persecute everyone that is serious about following God. It's important to realize that such persecution may take many forms. Looking at the verses above from II Timothy, we see Paul describing his ministry for the Lord. Those ministry opportunities led him into persecution in three different cities.

Paul indicates that he did not cease to make known the doctrine that led to right living, right thinking, and right motives. He indicates that he ministered under the influence of the Spirit with faith, longsuffering, charity (love) and patience. In other words, as Paul ministered, he followed God's system of management to deal with circumstances and the shortcomings of others.

Despite doing what was right, or rather, because of doing what was right, Paul listed three different places where he had suffered persecution: Antioch, Iconium, and Lystra. But what happened to Paul in each of those places was very different. So let's look at the different kind of persecutions Paul suffered.

Persecution in Antioch

"And the next Sabbath day came **almost the whole city together to hear the word of God.** But when the Jews saw the multitudes, **they were filled with envy,** and spake against those things which were spoken by Paul, contradicting and blaspheming."-Acts 13:44-45

Here we see Paul being contradicted and blasphemed by the Jewish religious leaders because of their jealousy. Why were they jealous? Because Paul was effective at reaching a crowd—almost the whole city came out to hear him preach. Paul was effective because he did things the right way, according to God's system of management.

As a result, he and Barnabas experienced criticism and disagreements with the Jewish people who loved God but did not believe in Jesus as the Messiah. They threw nothing but verbal insults and attacks. There were no stones or physical assaults. Yet Paul referred to simple verbal abuse as persecution!

He could have responded by quitting the ministry. He could have ceased submitting to the Spirit's leading and brought an end to the persecution by being silent. Instead Paul responded under the influence of the fruit of the Spirit—Peace. The next verse says they "waxed bold" meaning they grew in courage in the face of their verbal persecutions.

Since Paul knew God was in control, he knew that he was safe from harm in his spirit, mind and body. His spirit—his temperament—refers to the seat of his passions. Paul's *spirit* didn't get emotional about being in harm's way. He didn't fret in his *mind* or fear for the protection of his *body*. He responded by continuing to minister, as God led, to the Gentiles instead of the Jews.

Acts 13:46 says, "Then Paul and Barnabas waxed bold, and said, It was necessary that the word of God should first have been spoken to you: but seeing ye put it from you, and judge yourselves unworthy of everlasting life, lo, we turn to the Gentiles." What if Paul had not loved those to whom he ministered with joy, experiencing great peace as a result?

He could have *selfishly* focused on his own benefit, and responded with *frustration*, thereby missing God's plan for his life. Instead he lived godly in Christ Jesus. Under the Spirit's influence, he suffered a non-physical persecution—pursuit of oppression—by jealous religious leaders. He continued to minister under the influence of the peace of God.

Persecution at Iconium

"And it came to pass in Iconium, that they went both together into the synagogue of the Jews, and so spake, that a great multitude both of the Jews and also of the Greeks believed. But the unbelieving Jews stirred up the Gentiles, and made their minds evil affected against the brethren. Long time therefore abode they speaking boldly in the Lord, which gave testimony unto the word of his grace, and granted signs and wonders to be done by their hands. But the multitude of the city was divided: and part held with the Jews, and part with the apostles. And when there was an assault made both of the Gentiles, and also of the Jews with their rulers, to use them despitefully, and to stone them, They were ware of it, and fled unto Lystra and Derbe, cities of Lycaonia, and unto the region that lieth round about: And there they preached the gospel."-Acts 14:1-7

Here we see what the Bible describes as a "stirring up" of the Gentiles by the Jews. Again, the focus of opposition to the ministry of Paul and Barnabas was their effectiveness. Many Jews and Greeks believed their message. This time the persecution was more serious. There still were angry words, but this time there was also the threat of physical violence.

The unbelieving Jews incited the Gentiles (it was too late for them to persuade the believing Jews!) and instigated a tumult against Paul and Barnabas by poisoning the minds of the people with criticism against them. This is yet another example of verbal persecution—a pursuit of oppression—against Spirit-led believers. But it falls short of physical injury!

Again, Paul responded with peace. This time, though, his response went in a different direction. Because of the effectiveness of their ministry, he and Barnabas decided not only to stay in Iconium, but to also continue speaking boldly. The Bible says, "**Long time** therefore abode they **speaking boldly** in the Lord." The peace that is the fruit of the Spirit helped them face persecution without worry, much less fear. Consequently, God's power became even more evident as He granted these godly men the ability to perform signs and wonders.

God's hand was on the ministry of Paul and Barnabas, despite their verbal persecutions. They stood strong and responded to criticism and attacks with the fruit of the Spirit—Peace. It was manifested by their boldness. But things continued to get worse. The people became divided; unbelievers against believers. Things reached a boiling point when the Jews encouraged the Gentiles "to use them despitefully."

That literally means a "reproach that attempts physical injury." The conflict had grown from verbal criticism to verbal confrontation to a threat of real injury. The mob wanted to stone them for what the Jewish leaders considered blasphemy. Paul responded the same way that Jesus did when He faced a similar threat—he left in a hurry.

The fruit of the Spirit—Peace led Paul and Barnabas to retreat rather staying and triggering a riot between the believers and unbelievers. What was God doing while this was going on? What was His purpose behind the persecution? Acts 16:1 says, "Then came he to Derbe and Lystra: and behold, a certain disciple was there, named Timotheus, the son of a certain woman, which was a Jewess, and believed; but his father was a Greek."

As a result of the stalled work in Iconium, and the physical pursuit of oppression, Paul and Barnabas went to Lyconia and met young Timothy. What a blessing and benefit Timothy would prove to be to those persecuted preachers! God knew exactly what He was doing. And Paul and Barnabas trusted in His wisdom and goodness while exhibiting the fruit of peace in the face of pursuing oppression—persecution. Now what happened next?

<u>Persecution at Lystra</u>

"And there came thither certain Jews from Antioch and Iconium, who persuaded the people, and, having stoned Paul, drew him out of the city, supposing he had been dead. Howbeit, as the disciples stood round about him, he rose up, and came into the city, and the next day he departed with Barnabas to Derbe. And…they…preached the gospel to that city, and had taught many."-Acts 14:19-21

The same troublemakers from Antioch and Iconium caught up with Paul? This time his persecution was physical in its nature. They stoned him! Surely Paul, would lose his peace from the Spirit now? But no, he did not fear them, even after he had been stoned and left for dead. When he revived, he went right back into the city and preached again. What an unbelievable measure of peace God gave Paul! He was so free from worry of harm to his spirit, mind and body that he had no fear of man.

Acts 19:21-22 says, "They returned again to Lystra, and to Iconium, and Antioch, Confirming the souls of the disciples, and exhorting them to continue in the faith, and that we must through much tribulation enter into the kingdom of God." Unbelievable! They jumped from the frying pan into the fire! They went back to the very same places where they had suffered persecution, both verbal and physical. There they encouraged fellow Christians to continue in their bold belief in God's system of management (faith).

How does Paul's instruction to Timothy regarding peace in the face of persecution conclude? He said, "But evil men and seducers shall wax worse and worse, deceiving, and being deceived. But continue thou in the things which thou hast learned and hast been assured of, knowing of whom thou hast learned them." (II Tim. 3:13-14)

Paul told Timothy (and us) what to expect if we live a godly life under the influence of Christ—persecution. You will suffer pursuits of oppression from people you try to help. It may be verbal, whether to your face or behind your back. Or it may be a physical persecution. Whatever kind of persecution you face, if you respond properly, God's power will be on your life.

Do not worry, and do not retaliate. Plunge instead into God's perfect peace and boldly continue what God leads you to do. You can trust Him for deliverance. Below is part of a song that eloquently reminds us of the truth of God's ability to protect us in times of persecution and adversity.

God on the Mountain (Tracy Darrt)
Life is easy when you're up on the mountain
And you've got peace of mind like you've never known.
But when things change and you're down in the valley,
Don't lose faith for you're never alone

For the God on the mountain is still God in the valley,
When things go wrong, He'll make it right.
And the God of the good times is still God in the bad times,
The God of the day is still God in the night.

We Often Prefer the Work of the Flesh—Worry

There is nothing more attractive to a lost person than someone who loves unconditionally, expresses great joy in life's adversities, and exhibits a peace that surpasses understanding in the face of opposition. At the same time, there is nothing more hypocritical to a lost person than self-centered, frustrated people who call themselves Christians.

It is very possible for Christians to be like that when they are living under the influence of the soul rather than the Spirit. Such people, however, will not only fail to experience the joy of the Lord, but they also will not experience the fruit of the Spirit—peace. They certainly will not feel free from fear of harm in spirit, mind and body.

Instead they settle for the alternative the devil offers, the work of the flesh called worry. Worry means "to live in fear of harm in your spirit, mind, and body." Worry is a poor testimony to those who are observing our walk with the Lord. I have met many Christians who live much of their lives worrying about things.

I am guilty, at times, to yielding to my soul's fear of harm as well. I believe the reason we struggle with worry is because our good works are sometimes done under an influence other than the influence of Christ. The difference between living in peace and living in worry is found in our perspective.

God is the true judge of what is good for us. He will never harm us. Everything is going to work together for our good. The persecutions of life will never bring us harm in God's eyes. However our outward man tends to look at our circumstances as potentially harmful. This is a lack of faith based on a wrong perspective. The inward man knows the promises of Scripture cannot be broken.

If our perspective is from the inner man, we will realize that God will never harm us. We may view a painful experience as harmful, but God does not. He views what happens as good for us. We are completely safe from harm. To this end, whenever you are faced with persecution, we must remember to look at every circumstance "in Christ Jesus."

The Holy Spirit will always lead us to be at peace; to trust God and have faith in Him and His Word. When we do, we can respond to any persecution or adversity without a shred of worry. Do you worry that God may take your spouse or your child? Do you worry that God may take your job or your home? Do you worry about things that might happen that you feel would cause you harm? That simply means you're human.

I don't for a minute mean to suggest that these are not terrible things to endure. I am simply saying if God allows them in your life, they are not going to bring you harm in God's eyes. And if

THERE IS NOTHING MORE ATTRACTIVE TO A LOST PERSON THAN SOMEONE WHO LOVES UNCONDITIONALLY, EXPRESSES GREAT JOY IN LIFE'S ADVERSITIES, AND EXHIBITS A PEACE THAT SURPASSES UNDERSTANDING IN THE FACE OF OPPOSITION.

you are yielded to the Holy Spirit and walking after Him, they will not bring you harm in your eyes either.

I am not trafficking in un-lived truths here. I have personally experienced this blessed truth in my life. I have failed to experience it at others times, for the very reasons listed above. But this one thing is sure: when we experience such situations, we find that we can respond properly by yielding to the Holy Spirit.

I refer to these first three fruits of the Spirit—love, joy and peace—as "inner being transformation" because Romans 12:2 teaches us that transformation must come before conformation. We cannot change the way we act until we change the way we think. God must first change the inside of man. The devil begins his work on the outside. He uses outside influences of the lust of the flesh to prey on the mind; the lust of the eyes to prey on the will; and the pride of life to prey on the emotions.

The devil's work begins on the outside and tries to destroy us on the inside. God works from the inside out. The inner man is the part of man that communicates with God. The Spirit influences the inner man, and when we yield to that influence, it always conforms our outer being to the image of Christ.

Next we'll look at the second three fruits of the Spirit—the ones I refer to as "outer being conformation."

chapter four

LONGSUFFERING VS. QUICK-TEMPERED

LONGSUFFERING IS THE FIRST OF THE THREE FRUITS THAT AFFECT OUR OUTER MAN—THE WAY WE BEHAVE TOWARD OTHERS. For me personally, this is one of the most difficult fruits to yield to. When I do respond properly with longsuffering, I am certainly aware of the fact that God is doing the work instead of me! Longsuffering is defined as "an enduring temperament that expresses itself in patience with the shortcomings of others."

Let's dissect that definition. *Temperament* refers to a person's makeup— the passions, attitudes, and other elements of temper that combine to produce a level of irritability, whether high or low. *Enduring means* "to continue without perishing" or "to last long, even to permanence." *Patience means* "calm in temper." Thus, longsuffering is the combination of attitudes that expresses itself in long, lasting calmness.

To whom is this combination of attitudes to be expressed? Well, by definition, that spirit of calmness should be expressed toward people who have shortcomings. *Short* means "not of sufficient length" and *comings* means "to advance toward a target."

God Offers the Fruit of the Spirit – Longsuffering

I've given you a rather lengthy definition of longsuffering, but I think it's important to show how God intends for us to respond to others who fail to reach our expectations and targets. We all have expectations of what other people should be doing and how they should be acting. Too often we feel let down by people.

Regardless of whether they were wrong in falling short or whether our expectations were unrealistic, God's intention is for us to respond with the fruit of the Spirit—longsuffering. He wants us to respond with an enduring temperament expressed by patience with the shortcomings or faults of others.

As we look back at the fruits of the Spirit we've studied to this point, we see how each fruit flows from the previous one. When we love people without expectation of return, we experience rejoicing in all circumstances. That joy leads to a peaceful freedom from worry in mind, body and spirit. To this point we see an individual who is personally responding properly to every circumstance of life.

If the devil fails to influence us to self-love, frustration, or worry, he will work on others whom he can influence to act in a fleshly manner *toward us*. His goal is the same—to influence us away from yielding to the Holy Spirit. He works to sway people to fall short of our expectations. The more that we are doing for others, the easier it is for them to either knowingly or unknowingly let us down.

What good does it do to respond properly to the needs of others, to express joy in difficult circumstances, and to rest in absolute peace in the face of oppression only to react in a fleshly manner toward those we are trying to help? That makes no sense! Yet sometimes the more we allow proper responses to flow through us from the Holy Spirit, the more we expect from others. After all if we can yield to the Spirit's leading, is it too much to demand the same of others, especially those who are benefiting from our godly responses? In a word, yes.

If you place such expectations on others, you are setting yourself up for failure. Many times I've heard pastors tell how they have helped hurting people in their churches. They have poured their hearts into their preaching and their counseling, offering encouragement and providing for personal needs. Yet those people in whom they have invested so much turn around and let them down. They frequently leave the church without a word of thanks. In fact, they often exit spewing insults and trying to take others with them.

I believe this is a direct result of the spiritual warfare each of us face. The devil knows that the best witness is a person who is lifting up Jesus Christ. When He is lifted up, people are drawn to Him. (John 12:32) When we respond properly and show the fruit of the Spirit, we make Jesus look good and bring glory to God. Our inner man shines through and influences others. Satan's goal is to hide the light of the truth, because light destroys the kingdom of darkness.

"But if our gospel be hid, it is hid to them that are lost: In whom the god of this world hath blinded the minds of them which believe not, lest the light of the glorious gospel of Christ, who is the image of God, should shine unto them…For God, who commanded the light to shine out of darkness, hath shined in our hearts, to give the light of the knowledge of the glory of God in the face of Jesus Christ. But we have this treasure in earthen vessels, that the excellency of the power may be of God, and not of us. We are troubled on every side, yet not distressed; we are perplexed, but not in despair; Persecuted, but not forsaken; cast

THUS FOR A CHRISTIAN, ATTACKS, TROUBLES, DISAPPOINTMENTS AND PERSECUTION SHOULD BE VIEWED AS OPPORTUNITIES TO WITNESS THROUGH OUR LONGSUFFERING.

down, but not destroyed; Always bearing about in the body the dying of the Lord Jesus, that the life also of Jesus might be made manifest in our body."-II Corinthians 4:3-10

The devil's plan to hide the light of God's truth from the lost is frustrated when we respond to life's circumstances with longsuffering rather than a quick-temper. When others see God's image in us, the light of the Gospel shines in the darkness. Thus for a Christian, attacks, troubles, disappointments and persecution should be viewed as opportunities to witness through our longsuffering.

When we respond according to God's Spirit, those around us will not see the fleshly responses they expect—anger, frustration and worry. When we do not walk after the Spirit in our responses, we are hiding our light under a bushel. (Luke 11:33) Many people read Jesus' words and think He is talking about people who are afraid to witness.

That is partly true, but we hide our candle far more often with our outer man—refusing to let the Spirit dictate our response to circumstances than we do by fear of speaking out. It is usually our inconsistency in yielding to the Spirit that leaves us embarrassed and unwilling to share our faith. The truth is that there is no other fruit of the Spirit that leads more people to Christ than the fruit of longsuffering in the face of disappointment in others.

God showed that same spirit toward us before we were saved. His light showed patiently in such a way that our minds were changed from unbelief to faith in Jesus Christ. Paul wrote, "And thinkest thou this, O man, that judgest them which do such things, and doest the same, that thou shalt escape the judgment of God? Or despiseth thou the riches of his goodness and forbearance and longsuffering; not knowing that the goodness of God leadeth thee to repentance?" (Rom. 2:3-4)

In these verses we are reminded of how easy it is for us to condemn those who fall short of our expectations. Yet often, even as we judge others, we are guilty of the very same shortcomings. We overlook the fact that God's longsuffering response to our failures is what leads us to repentance.

Could God strike us down on the spot every time we do wrong? Of course He could. In fact, He would be justified in doing so. Yet his calm response to our sins brings us great benefits because of His longsuffering. But in our relations with others, we often do not show that same restraint. Instead we harshly judge those who disappoint us. According to Romans 2:1, this behavior is "inexcusable."

God's longsuffering toward us is both a pattern for us to follow and a motivation for us to respond properly to the shortcomings of others. Satan knows that if we respond to disappointments in the flesh, he can succeed in hiding the light of the Gospel from shining through our lives to others.

So if he fails to get us to respond in the flesh to adversity, his next step is often to influence others to let us down. That is when it is most critical that we respond under the influence of the Spirit with the fruit of longsuffering. The devil's alternative to longsuffering is much more satisfying to the flesh. He encourages us to a reactionary work of the flesh that I call a quick-tempered response.

We Often Prefer the Work of the Flesh—Quick Tempered

Temper refers to the seat of our passions and desires. It is the root from which we get the word temperament, which we've seen means "a combination of passions that produces a level of irritability or contentment." Being quick-tempered indicates that it takes very little to excite our passions in a negative way.

As I mentioned, even after more than three decades as a believer, I am just now learning how to yield to this fruit of the Spirit. That's because I have resisted it. As a result, I have hindered God's work in my life. For years I failed to see the connection between my temper and my reluctance to do the things God called me to do. Simply put, I was afraid to serve God because of my shame at the way I reacted to people.

Before I came back to Christ in 1993, I was an unproductive disappointment to many people who had invested in me. My parents, after sacrificing for ten years to invest in a Christian education for me, watched with sadness as I went out into the world and rejected the Spirit-led lifestyle. Yet they always responded in a loving, longsuffering way.

My employers, seeing great potential in me, invested in training and preparing me for positions of influence in their businesses. Despite those efforts, I never met their expectations, and never lived up to my potential. Eventually I had a resume so poor that it left me basically unemployable. Having rejected my Christian upbringing, I settled for a self-satisfying lifestyle that led to drugs, alcohol, and other crippling, sinful habits.

Throughout this time, I received longsuffering responses from God. I had a list of grievances a mile long (it's ridiculous to look back at that list now) against my parents, my pastor, my teachers, my employers and the government. Then came an almost fatal car wreck.

Someone asked me later about my accident, and I told them that while I had indeed been in a wreck, *it was no accident*. It was the mercy of God opening my eyes to the potential end result of the life I was living. As I lay in the hospital bed reading the Gospel of John, my eyes were opened to the sufferings my shortcomings were causing to other people in my life.

I repented of the way I had taken advantage of the longsuffering responses of those who had tried to help me. I realized that if I continued to take advantage of them, God was going to bring my life to an end. He began to work in my heart to establish a healthy fear of the Lord, and a genuine spirit of gratitude toward those who were trying to help me.

When I got out of the hospital, my life began to change very quickly as a direct result of my repentance and new attitude. I became very productive at my job; I began to grow in my spiritual life; and I became effective in service to God at my church. From that point forward, it seemed like everything I did went well.

It was a very exciting and enjoyable time in my life. I was gaining favor with God, and He was giving me favor with man. In a few short years, I went from being one of the most unproductive Christians alive to being an executive in the oil business and then promoted to being a full-time servant of God in the ministry of Reformers Unanimous International.

But for all of the good things that happened and all of the changes I experienced, there was one work of the flesh that remained strong in my life. Everyone who worked under me, with me, or over me became aware that I was quick-tempered. I had developed a habit of responding to people in this flesh when they disappointed me.

I'm telling you my story in the hope that it will open your eyes to how the devil works in your life to keep you in bondage. As I told you,

I had spent nearly all of my life being unproductive. I was a serious disappointment to those in authority over me. When I gave my life back to God, however, He began to bless me in a great way. Seeing the change in productivity in my life, I increased my expectations for myself.

What I failed to realize was that the increased productivity was not my own doing, but rather God working in me. At the same time I raised my expectations of myself, I also raised my expectations of others. Shamefully, I was not willing to do for others what God had done for me for so long. I became obsessed with attaining a level of productivity that was so high that no one was able to produce at a level that satisfied me.

I expected a level of perfection from my wife as a wife and mother that I was unable to meet as a husband and father. Though my staff worked long hours, I often reprimanded them for failing to live up to my standards. I became overbearing. I placed heavy and unscriptural burdens on my family, my staff, and even our ministry volunteers.

I was reacting after the flesh to what I perceived as the shortcomings of others. Though I had never exhibited this fleshy counterfeit to the fruit of the Spirit in the days when I was failing in every area of my life, I began to exhibit it toward others on a regular basis. I took up the evil temperament of being quick-tempered toward those who I thought were letting me down. What a sad testimony for a Christian leader!

For the first several years of our ministry, I did not realize my error. It was not until God led me to write and teach on anger that I began to see I had a serious problem. I found that after I had studied and written a message, I was unable to deliver it. I knew that if I stood and preached that message that I would be a complete hypocrite.

When I found myself unable to teach something that God was clearly leading me to teach, I came face to face with my failure to walk after His Spirit. I realized that I was putting expectations on people that God did not put on them (or on me). Yet I found that despite the fact that I was being quick-tempered, God was still being longsuffering toward me. His goodness in response to my sinfulness was very convicting, and led me to repentance.

It was only a year ago that this lesson came to me. To the glory of God, I am working toward a complete 180 degree turnaround. I am not out of the woods when it comes to my fleshly desires to react with a quick temper, but God has given me the grace to recognize this flaw.

I had people quit over the pressure of working for me. I had people distance themselves from their relationship with me because of my temper. I had students who quit the program because they couldn't measure up to my standards. None of these things convinced me to change.

It was only when I realized that my fleshy reaction was hindering God's ability to speak through me that I realized my sin. My light was shining less and less. In my zeal to increase productivity, I actually became less productive! The devil knows that if he cannot hinder your productivity by getting you to

OUR WILLINGNESS TO BE PATIENT WITH PEOPLE WHEN THEY DISAPPOINT US MAKES GOD LOOK GOOD, BECAUSE THAT IS NOT A NATURAL HUMAN RESPONSE.

be selfish, frustrated, or worried, he may succeed in getting you to be proud of your own productivity, and quick-tempered toward others. Nothing interferes with the productivity of God like the pride of man.

If you struggle with this work of the flesh, I encourage you to memorize and meditate on Proverbs 19:11. It says, "The discretion (proper judgment) of a man deferreth (delays) his anger; and it is his glory to pass over (overlook) a transgression (violation)." Proper judgment helps us delay our anger at those who let us down.

The thing about delayed anger is that it disperses. After time passes, we can overlook the disappointment we feel all together. Our willingness to be patient with people when they disappoint us makes God look good, because that is not a natural human response. By yielding to the Spirit, we will be able to suffer for a long time with the shortcomings of others. The inner man will flow through, and God will receive glory as He lives through us.

chapter five

GENTLENESS VS. HARSHNESS

THE BIBLE WORD "GENTLENESS" MEANS SOFTNESS IN MANNERS. SOFTNESS, COUPLED WITH MANNERS GIVES US THE CONCEPT OF MILDNESS. Our manners are the way in which we interact in our duties of life, behavior, demeanor, conduct, and management. In other words, we could describe gentleness as being mild-mannered.

Do you know people whose manners are soft and genteel? Of course we are not talking about having good manners at the dinner table (although that is certainly important). We are talking about a manner of mildness as we face our day to day responsibilities. Mild can also mean tender. Thus a person who is under the influence of the Spirit will act and respond in a tender and mannerly way.

God Offers the Fruit of the Spirit—Gentleness

There are people in my life who excel in yielding to a particular fruit. When I think of the fruit of gentleness, I am reminded of my pastor, Dr. Paul Kingsbury. He is the gentlest man I have ever met. He is mild in every area of his life. Dr. Kingsbury is the father of twelve children. He pastors a church of about a thousand members. He is the board chairman of Reformers Unanimous International.

As you can see, he is busy. He may be the busiest man I know. Yet despite his busyness, he is always joyful, kind, considerate, patient and willing to listen to anyone who approaches him with a problem. His daughter Joy works for our ministry. Recently when I was out of town, she called me. Her younger brother Joey had just been diagnosed with leukemia. This young man had graduated from high school only one month earlier.

Her father was also out of town and would not be able to get home for five days. When he returned home, he was faced with even more tragedy. One of the deacons, a pillar of the church, had been diagnosed with cancer. He had been given just four weeks to live. The following day, a married couple from the church was involved in a motorcycle accident, and the wife was killed.

I arrived home in time to attend the Wednesday night service. For most of the congregation, it was the first time they had heard about these three difficult situations. Oh how oppressed I felt that evening! But as I watched our pastor as he led the service in testimonies and prayer, I was amazed at his gentle manner. I watched him listen intently to many prayer requests that paled in comparison to the heartaches he was facing. He preached with a soft spirit and with all his heart.

After the service, I stood in line in the auditorium to speak to him. As I waited while he talked with the final few people ahead of me, I overheard what each of them were talking to him about. I observed as these people brought their petty problems to him without any regard for the burdens he was carrying that evening. Yet the whole time he looked them in the eye, listened and smiled, and committed to help them. He made notes of things he would be doing to help members who were piling more of their personal problems onto his current load.

When he approached me, he smiled even more broadly. Before I could offer him my condolences for the sorrowful circumstances, he rushed up and gave me a hug and told me how much he had missed me. He then asked me to give him an update on the ministry all the problems we were having! Wow! Talk about big shoulders!

That is a true man of God. How does he keep his cool? It's simple— he doesn't! The Holy Spirit of God is working as Dr. Kingsbury yields to Him to produce the fruit of gentleness in his life. When confronted with adversity, he faces his responsibilities and conducts himself in a tenderly mannered way. That is the power of Christ acting and responding through him.

I have asked my pastor how he is able to be so mild mannered toward people. He told me that his ability to respond to his day-to-day duties under the influence of the fruit of the Spirit—gentleness is a result off his decision to forgive people for their insensitivities. As a result of his example, I am learning this long lesson as well.

At times I do struggle with the three fruits that deal with conformity of the outer man: longsuffering, gentleness and goodness. A few years ago, I began taking steps of action to offset my struggle to yield to the fruit of the Spirit—gentleness. Not that I have completely attained, but I have learned a lot about God's ability to handle my problems and discouragements.

Some time ago, I started to become abrasive when dealing with my responsibilities in counseling fallen students. I place much effort into each of my students, and love them dearly. I struggle when I see them fall, and when they do, I want to help them. However, with some, it seems that after they fall, they want to talk about their problems instead of doing something about them.

I want to be a good steward, and not allow my time to be abused by those who are not serious about recovery. I had a few students who began to fall somewhat regularly. I had placed a great deal of time into counseling and teaching them. Over and over again, they would call and ask, "Wondered if you have a few minutes?" "Of course I do," I would always reply.

When they would arrive, they would give me the news. We would cry, talk, cry, and pray. I would encourage them. It seemed to do no good. Over and over again, they would fall and call; fall and call. This went on for about five months. I got to the point where I was anything but gentle in my daily duties.

I would come to work in the morning discouraged. I would look at my schedule and see the same names over and over again. To top it off, after some students would fall away and stop asking for help, their slots on my schedule would be filled by new students who had been doing well but now were not. Oh the frustration I felt! It showed in my mannerisms.

When my secretary would tell me an appointment had arrived, I would roll my eyes and think, "Here we go again." I was critical and negative toward the repeat offenders. I was harsh and unkind to those who did not follow my counsel quickly and correctly. I was not pleasant to work with, and I was not pleasant to counsel with. My motives were good—I wanted a ministry that was successful in helping people rather than one that was steeped in daily defeats. I wanted our students to only experience a victory that was sustainable and enjoyable.

I realized I had a problem one day when I was counseling a woman who was bitter at her husband for his continual defeat on his road to recovery. She was mean to him, often unrelenting in her personal criticism of his shortcomings. I took her to the book of Ephesians to show her how she needed to respond to her husband's failures.

While I was reading these verses to her, I realized what was causing me to refuse to yield to gentleness. In fact, I was so struck by conviction that I had to excuse myself from our meeting. I asked God to help me do what I was sharing with her from the Scriptures in my own life. What were those verses that God used to change my behavior?

The Bible says, "Let all bitterness, and wrath, and anger, and clamour, and evil speaking, be put away from you, with all malice: And be ye kind one to another, tenderhearted, forgiving one another, even as God for Christ's sake hath forgiven you." (Eph. 4:31-32) That means I am to forgive anyone who hurts me in any way, no matter what they have done, or how often they do it.

My friend, that is the key ingredient that will release you from the fleshly alternative to gentleness. Forgiveness will allow you to respond in a mild mannered, tender and gentle way to your day, your duties, and your disappointments. It is not a sin to be disappointed; it is a sin to allow that disappointment to cause you to yield to a work of the flesh. Let's dissect and define these verses and see just what it teaches.

bitterness: compressed feelings
wrath: feelings of getting even
anger: passions of the mind
clamour: argumentativeness
evil speaking: gossiping
malice: desire for physical injury
kind: outward demonstration of gentleness
tenderhearted: inward demonstration of gentleness
forgiving: upward demonstration of gentleness

God's Word shows us that forgiveness—true forgiveness, produces mild mannered responses. The opposite of that kind of response (the one I had fallen into the trap of displaying toward my students) is the work of the flesh—Harshness.

We Often Prefer the Work of the Flesh—Harshness

The list of fleshly reactions in Ephesians 4:31 is the way most people react when they feel someone has violated them. It is the antithesis of gentleness. If we fight back, tell others off, argue, get violently passionate, attempt to get revenge, or even suppress our feelings and do nothing about them, we are not yielding to the Holy Spirit. Instead we are exercising the work of the flesh—harshness.

The dictionary defines harshness as a "roughness in manner,

temper, or words." The desire to respond with harshness can cause us to dislike everybody and everything in our relationships and responsibilities. If we act on that desire, it will cause others to hate everything about us. Harsh personalities are not enjoyed; instead they are destroyed. Either they self-destruct or they are avoided by others to the extent that relationships and careers are damaged.

David said, "Thou hast also given me the shield of thy salvation: and thy right hand hath holden me up, and thy gentleness hath made me great." (Ps. 18:35) The fruit of the Spirit—Gentleness will lead others to consider you a great person to be around. Harsh people are never considered great guys or great gals.

God wants us to respond in a gentle way when we deal with difficult people or circumstances. Gentleness is especially important when the problem we are having is caused by the failure of others. If we yield to His leading, we will always respond gently rather than harshly.

In James 3:17, we see that when God gives us wisdom and direction, it comes with some uniquely tender responses. "But the wisdom that is from above is first pure, then peaceable, **gentle**, and easy to be entreated, full of mercy and good fruits, without partiality, and without hypocrisy."

That's a far cry from the way I was responding to the people who were falling and calling on me for help. Was my problem because I wasn't asking for God's help in responding properly? No, my harshness was a direct result of being offended. I was upset that I had worked so hard to help them and felt they were letting me down. I was taking their failures personally, and it was destroying my moods and manners.

Listen to what Paul said to Timothy.

"And the servant of the Lord must not strive; but be gentle unto all men, apt to teach, patient, In meekness instructing those that oppose themselves; if God peradventure will give them repentance in the acknowledging of the truth; And that they may recover themselves out of the snare of the devil, who are taken captive by him at his will." -II Tim. 2:24-26

To strive means "to put forth great effort." The Bible is telling us that we should not have to work hard, but rather be apt, or willing, to teach in a gentle, patient fashion. Surely if God expects us to teach in a gentle fashion without having to work hard, it must mean that people will be easy to work with…Nope! In fact the Scripture says that we must gently teach "those that oppose themselves." This is talking about those who do great harm to themselves without caring whether they follow our teaching or not.

Such people are snared by the devil and in captivity to him. Now I don't know about you, but responding gently to people like that seems impossible to me. It would seem that they would require the *most* effort, the *most* striving. Yet if we are willing to teach them in a patient and gentle fashion, then we won't have to work hard to keep them. We might even lead them to the position of repentance that will bring them out of captivity!

How do we do this? How do we stop trying hard and instead yield to the Spirit's fruit of gentleness? The only way to do that is by forgiving people in the manner that Paul describes in Ephesians 4:32. To do that, we really follow his list in reverse order. If we start with bitterness, we may never forgive; but if we start with forgiveness, we will never be bitter.

To show an outward demonstration of gentleness—to be kind to one another—we must begin by forgiving the perpetrator. We will never be kind to others until we forgive them. God knows our hearts. If we don't ask Him to give us the grace to forgive them, then we will never receive the benefit of having a forgiving heart. That benefit is the second step to gentle response—having a tender heart.

If we forgive, then we experience the tender heart that we need in order to reach the third step of a gentle response—being kind to one another. Titus 3:1-2 says, "Put them in mind (remind them) to be subject to principalities and powers, to obey magistrates, to be ready to every good work, To speak evil of no man, to be no brawlers, but **gentle**, shewing all meekness unto all men."

chapter six

GOODNESS VS. MEANNESS

SOME PEOPLE THINK THAT THE FRUIT WE JUST STUDIED, GENTLENESS, IS IDENTICAL TO THE FRUIT OF GOODNESS. It is true that there are similarities between them, but they are different responses toward different circumstances in life.

Gentleness is a reaction that we demonstrate by yielding to God. Goodness, like love, is an action. The Bible definition of goodness is "conforming our lives and conversations to behave benevolently toward others." Goodness only happens when we allow a conformation (a pouring into a mold) to take place in our lives. The mold that we are being poured into will produce benevolent behavior on our part in both word and deed.

God Offers the Fruit of the Spirit—Goodness

How does goodness manifest itself in our behavior? We manifest goodness when we are benevolent toward others. In fact, benevolence is a synonym for goodness. Webster's 1868 Dictionary defines benevolent as "having a disposition to do good; possessing a love for mankind, and a desire to promote their prosperity and happiness."

Benevolence then describes a person who seeks to promote prosperity and happiness in the lives of others. By the way, that's the kind of person the world would consider to be a "good" person. But for Christians, true goodness comes as we yield to the fruit of the Holy Spirit. Spirit led Christians are molded to act in such a way that they promote happiness and prosperity toward everyone.

As with all good traits, God is the perfect example of goodness.

"Oh how great is thy goodness, which thou hast laid up for them that fear thee; which thou hast wrought for them that trust in thee before the sons of men!" Psalm 31:19

"Oh that men would praise the Lord for his goodness, and for his wonderful works to the children of men! For he satisfieth the longing soul, and filleth the hungry soul with goodness." Psalm 107:8-9

"And Jethro rejoiced for all the goodness which the Lord had done in Israel, whom he had delivered out of the hand of the Egyptians." II Chronicles 7:10 says, "And on the three and twentieth day of the seventh month he sent the people away into their tents, glad and merry in heart for the goodness that the Lord had shewed unto David, and to Solomon, and to Israel his people." Exodus 8:9

There are enough verses in the Old and New Testaments about God's unending and undeserved goodness toward us to fill this entire book with examples. Do you see how closely related goodness is to the transforming fruit of the Spirit—Love? Goodness is actually an outward demonstration of the inner yielding to the fruit of the Spirit—Love. Probably the best description of God's goodness toward us is found in the familiar words of Psalm 23.

"The Lord is my shepherd; I shall not want. He maketh me to lie down in green pastures: he leadeth me beside still waters. He restoreth my soul: he leadeth me in paths of righteousness for his name's sake. Yea, though I walk through the valley of the shadow of death, I will fear no evil: for thou art with me; thy rod and thy staff they comfort me. Thou preparest a table before me in the presence of mine enemies: thou anointest my head with oil; my cup runneth over. Surely goodness and mercy shall follow me all the days of my life: and I will dwell in the house of the Lord for ever." Psalm 23:1-6

David's statement shows us very clearly that God's goodness toward us is undeserved. Mercy is not getting what we deserve. By linking goodness and mercy, David is saying that, not only is he not getting what he deserves, he is getting God's goodness through no merit of his own.

I believe that an understanding of mercy is the primary catalyst for yielding to the Spirit that produces goodness. Goodness is allied when mercy is applied. It is God's mercy that leads Him to promote happiness and prosperity in our lives despite our failures and frustrations. God's mercy leads Him to be benevolent toward us.

Having received God's mercy ourselves, we must then extend that mercy toward others. Our willingness to yield to the inner man's desire, prompted by mercy, to show love will cause the outer man to conform his behavior to be benevolent. A heart of love produces an action of goodness.

Remember Romans 2:4? "The goodness of God leadeth thee to repentance." Goodness on our part is what encourages others to change their minds about the way they act. When they see goodness demonstrated toward them, it leads them to repentance. Thus the fruit of goodness is incredibly evangelistic!

Unfortunately for many of us, we struggle to yield to this fruit. I believe that struggle is directly related to our unwillingness to offer the response of mercy to others. We often prefer judgment over mercy. God never gives us permission to judge anyone but ourselves! Judgment is reserved for God; it is not for us.

Throughout Scripture, we are encouraged to demonstrate mercy. We are even told to offer grace; giving people what they don't deserve. God's command to demonstrate mercy and grace are seemingly tough demands when it comes to responding to those who have done us wrong. But consider this: if we are unforgiving, God will be unforgiving. If we do not show mercy, God will not show mercy to us. If we are not willing to give grace to others, God will withhold His grace from us.

One reason it is easy for us to prefer judging others to showing mercy is that it indulges a fleshly appetite. And that is the alternative the devil offers to the fruit of the Spirit—Goodness; the work of the flesh—Meanness.

We Often Prefer the Work of the Flesh—Meanness

When people hear the word "mean", they tend to think of someone who is angry, hateful, or vengeful. Those could be the attributes of someone who is mean-spirited, but that is not the type of meanness I'm talking about. You have probably heard the phrase "a man of many means" or its opposite, "a man of no means." The meanness that is the antithesis of the fruit of the Spirit—Goodness is "refusing to be liberal with charity, thus avoiding any personal expense."

These two contrasting types of behavior—being benevolent and being stingy—are often assumed to be only in the context of money. Either a person is a giver, or they are a hoarder. Of course in society that is obsessed with money, it is understandable to think of benevolence and charity as being the giving of financial resources. Yet there is much more to benevolence than simply giving away money.

For God's work to be done through men, He needs us to demonstrate goodness with our money, time, energies, gifts, and talents…and in our actions and reactions to the mistakes of others. God's work is hindered when we act or react to the failures of others refusing to share God's many resources that we have at our disposal.

How can we expect to advance the kingdom of God when our focus is on the acquisition of and the refusal to expend any valued resource for the sake of the "kingdom of me"? In the Sermon on the Mount, Jesus laid out what God thinks about choosing covetousness over benevolence. (Take time to read the whole passage so that our defining of Bible terms will be fully understood.)

"Lay not up for yourselves treasures upon earth, where moth and rust doth corrupt, and where thieves break through and steak: But lay up yourselves treasures in heaven, where neither moth nor rust doth corrupt, and where thieves do not break through nor steal: For where your treasure is, there will your heart be also. No man can serve two masters: for either he will hate the one, and love the other; or else he will hold to the one, and despise the others. Ye cannot serve God and mammon. Therefore I say unto you, Take no thought for your life, what ye shall eat, or what ye shall drink; nor yet for your body, what ye shall put on. Is not the life more than meat, and the body than raiment? Behold the fowls of the air: for they sow not, neither do they reap, nor gather into barns; yet your heavenly Father feedeth them. Are ye not much better than they? Which of you by taking thought can add one cubit unto his stature? And why take ye thought for raiment? Consider the lilies of the field, how they grow; they toil not, neither do they spin: And yet I say unto you, That even Solomon in all his glory was not arrayed like one of these. Wherefore, if God so clothe the grass of the field, which to day is, and to morrow is cast into the oven, shall he not much more clothe you, O ye of little faith? Therefore take no thought, saying, What shall we eat? or, What shall we drink? or, Wherewithal shall we be clothed? (For after all these things do the Gentiles seek:) for your heavenly Father knoweth that ye have need of all these things. But seek ye first the kingdom of God, and his righteousness; and all these things shall be added unto you."

Matthew 6:19-21, 24-33

Jesus tells us that we should not focus on the acquisition of temporary things that will be of no value to us when we die. Instead, we should lay up treasures in Heaven. The missionary martyr, Jim Elliott, said, "He is no fool who gives what he cannot keep to gain what he cannot lose." His focus was on eternal things.

The word treasure means a "great quantity of anything that is collected for future use." You might be tempted to think that laying things up for the future is the proper focus of life. But Jesus goes even further in telling us that we should not even worry about accumulating resources for day-to-day living! In our advanced society resources for daily living may not seem like a big deal, but in Jesus' day, that was the central focus of their lives.

Recently I spent some time in a third world country. In that time, I observed people struggling to survive. My wife and I established a friendship with a lady who braids the hair of travelers who come to her village. Speaking in broken English, she told us how her day begins at 8:00 AM and ends at 11:30 PM—seven days a week!

She works over one hundred hours a week! As she was braiding the hair of a young customer, it was nearing her quitting time. Her husband walked up to her stand, and began placing the beads in the little girl's hair to help his wife. He had been at work at the port since 6:00 AM!

I could not believe that they worked so hard and so long for so little. She told me that they do this to put food on the table for their three little girls. I was astonished that it took so much effort to provide the basic necessities of life—food, clothing and shelter. They were not working to acquire stuff; they were trying to provide for their survival. Their focus was on meeting their basic needs day by day and week by week.

In Jesus' day, there was no Wal-Mart on every street corner. There was no government aid, no unemployment insurance, no welfare, no return-to-work programs. So when Jesus told these people not to focus on necessary resources, He seemed to be telling them to abandon their existence! In reality, He was not teaching them to forsake the provision of their daily needs, but rather to get their focus off of that and onto the kingdom of God. When we do that, God provides every need often in abundance.

However, it is not enough to merely focus on the kingdom of God. There is another step to having our needs met here on earth. Jesus said that we must seek His righteousness. What does that mean? Remember that when we do good under the influence of the Spirit, we are engaged in righteousness. Therefore looking for opportunities to do good, under the influence of the Spirit (not doing good in our own power) is seeking God's righteousness.

In other words, to gain God's provision, we must experience justification and yield to our sanctification. God's desire is for people to accept Christ's sacrifice and to allow Him to lead them to reach others. Over and over again, Scripture confirms that this is God's plan for us. To accomplish this goal, He offers us the fruit of the Spirit—Goodness.

Naturally the devil tries to suppress the fruit of goodness by frustrating us and getting us to focus on meeting our own needs. This bumps God out of the equation. If we can meet our own needs, we will not learn to depend on God. God's tool of mercy is what creates a desire for Spirit-led believers to respond to the needy with goodness. Satan's tool of meanness gets fleshly-led believers to react to the needy with judgment.

God wants us to give the merciful response of goodness; the devil would have us give the judgmental reaction of meanness. The primary ministry of Reformers Unanimous is to impact the lives of the addicted with the gospel. Of course, as with any ministry, this kind of outreach requires benevolence on the part of God's people.

To see the lives of the addicted rebuilt, I must do what Nehemiah did when he wanted to rebuild the walls of Jerusalem. I must ask God to meet every need financially— **IF WE CAN MEET OUR OWN NEEDS, WE WILL NOT LEARN TO DEPEND ON GOD.** and then I must petition those whom God has given kingdom wealth to loosen their purse strings. I must request benevolence on the part of God's people.

I enjoy doing this because I get to minister to both the givers and receivers of the benevolence. It is a great privilege because there are often great needs on both sides of a gift. However, sometimes I come across people who are obviously in a position to give, yet whose reaction to my request show the undisguised work of the flesh—Meanness.

Let me explain why I believe this happens. I have always been told that working with addicted adults is an incredibly hard ministry for which to raise benevolence. I am also told that if I ran a ministry for battered women or underprivileged children I would have no problem raising money. It's hard to justify meanness to such victims.

But since I minister mainly to grown adults with self-inflicted problems, many potential givers justify their meanness (that is, they avoid personal expense by supplanting charity with judgment). They judge the needy to be unworthy of their merciful benevolence. That is not a godly response; it is a fleshly one. It is a sinful reaction.

Spirit-led believers have three possible responses to every request for benevolence. They can give, if the Spirit so leads, showing mercy while laying up treasure in Heaven. Or they can *not* give as the Spirit leads, or give elsewhere as the Spirit leads. Either way the choice should belong to the Spirit, not the soul of the giver. This type of giving gets it given back (Luke 6:38).

I don't know about you, but I don't want my treasure consumed by moths and stolen by thieves. By distributing benevolence with a heart of mercy to the undeserving, I know I will receive mercy from God, both on earth and in His Kingdom yet to come. As a child of God, the fruit of the Spirit—goodness is available to you.

I strongly encourage you to use it to benefit others. Let it be said of us even as Paul said of the church at Rome, "And I myself also am persuaded of you, my brethren, that ye also are **full of goodness**, filled with all knowledge, able also to admonish one another." (Rom. 15:14)

chapter seven

FAITH VS. DOUBT

THE FINAL THREE FRUITS OF THE SPIRIT DEAL WITH WHAT I CALL "NEW BEING REFORMATION." It should be evident by these final three fruits being yielded to and seen in our lives that we are indeed "new creatures" in Christ. (II Cor. 5:17)

Faith is completely crucial to every area of the Christian life. It is impossible to overstate the importance of this particular fruit of the Spirit. Justification from the penalty of sin and sanctification from the power of sin are both experienced by faith. We cannot please God without faith. (Heb. 11:6) We need faith because it is what allows believers to live freely in a bound world.

God Offers the Fruit of the Spirit—Faith

Faith is "a personal measurement of the level of confidence in what Christ has done and will do in, through and for us." All Christians have a personal measure of faith, and it should be evident in the life of a Spirit-led believer. Every victory in the Christian life is experienced as a direct result of the fruit of the Spirit—Faith. By contrast, every defeat in the Christian life is experienced as a directed result of the work of the flesh—Doubt.

I want you to see that justification is dependent upon faith in information, but the benefits of sanctification are dependent upon faith in a personal relation. When Eve responded improperly to the outside pressure of the possessed serpent, she did so because she doubted God's goodness to her. She thought God was holding something back from her. She wanted to know more information about God so that she could be like God.

Thus she ate of the Tree of Knowledge and plunged mankind into utter darkness. Since then, man has set off on a journey to know more about doing good in his own power, so that he may be like God. Man has rejected a personal relation for the acquisition of information. To this day, man assumes that knowledge is power, but it is not. Knowing God—on a personal level—is power.

In the Garden man knew God, but after the fall, man could no longer know God; he could only know *about* God. To satisfy man's penchant for knowing how to be like God, he was given information in the form of laws, commands, statutes, and judgments. This was intended to remove God's people from barbaric behavior and have a civilizing effect on them. The purpose of each covenant God made with man was to picture the day when the acquisition of information would become secondary to the development of a personal relation with Him.

That day came after Christ died and rose again. Since then, man can by faith accept Christ's atonement as payment for his sin, experiencing justification—freedom from the penalty of sin. Believers are new creatures who, though dead, live a new life in Christ through faith. The key verse for my

THE ONLY WAY TO LIVE A LIFE THAT IS DEAD TO SELF AND ALIVE IN CHRIST IS TO LIVE BY FAITH.

book *Nevertheless I Live: Living Freely in a Bound World* shows us this truth: "I am crucified with Christ: nevertheless I live; yet not I, but Christ liveth in me: and the life which I now live in the flesh I live by the faith of the Son of God, who loved me, and gave himself for me." (Gal. 2:20) We'll discuss this verse further in the final chapters of this book.

The only way to live a life that is dead to self and alive in Christ is to live by faith. Yielding daily to faith will allow God to work in our lives. This goes against our nature—it makes us feel uncomfortable to yield to faith in God. The Holy Spirit comes upon us to bring us help and guidance when we respond in faith. That is why Jesus called Him "the Comforter."

However we often run from the leading of faith and cling to the fleshly alternative of doubt. This causes us to make decisions based on information rather than on our personal relation with God. Romans 14:23 says, "Whatsoever is not of faith is sin." Any time we yield to doubt rather than to faith, we are sinning against God.

We Often Prefer the Work of the Flesh—Doubt

Too often, Christians actively doubt the truths of God's Word that we have been studying in this book. Although these truths are proven by personal experience as well as being reliable by virtue of being Scripture, we doubt them. That's because humanly speaking, doubt is easier to rationalize than faith is to internalize. The Bible meaning of doubt is "an attitude of unbelief, characterized by rebellion and disobedience to God."

By choosing the work of the flesh—Doubt in a given situation, we declare God to be a liar and presumptuously take control of our lives ourselves. Remember, the soul can be very convincing, and it always desires to be in control. The soul prefers to reject the boundaries of authority and choose instead to indulge in what the flesh thinks, wants, or feels. When we choose to doubt and reject taking the next step of faith as led by God, it is because we are yielding to one of the three aspects of the soul: mind, will or emotion.

Some fail to live by faith because they are mind driven. They doubt things because of intellectual reasoning. They are thinkers. There are churches that are focused too much on knowing *about* God because they are led by fleshly pastors who are driven by their minds. There are even entire denominations that are intellectually driven.

Another reason some fail to live by faith is because they are emotionally driven. They doubt what they know to be true because of the emotions that are created by doubt. The rejection of faith is more pleasing and acceptable to the flesh. There are churches that are focused way too much on emotionalism because they are led by fleshly pastors who are driven by their feelings. Again, there are whole denominations that are emotionally driven.

The third reason some fail to walk by faith is because they are driven by the desires of their will. They doubt certain truths because faith would keep them from doing what they want to do, or from doing things the way they want to do them. Their will is their master. There are churches that are led by fleshly pastors who are driven by their wills, placing huge burdens on God's laborers and refusing to allow change in any way. And there are denominations that are driven by strong-willed leadership.

This is the devil's design, not just for God's people in general, but specifically for pastors and church leaders. He knows that if he can get them to yield to the work of the flesh—Doubt, they will influence their followers to do so as well. When a church is led by fleshly pastors, the members will continue to struggle to yield to the fruit of the Spirit—Faith.

Here is the basic contrast between faith and doubt: When we yield to doubt, we are depending on desire, knowledge and reasoning to make our decisions. When we yield to faith, we are depending on God through our personal relation with Him to make our decisions.

This brings me to some final thoughts on the subject of faith. We often ask God to give us more faith. This is not a realistic request! We already have all the faith we need to live the victorious Christian life. When the disciples asked Jesus to increase their faith (Luke 17:5), He told them that faith the size of a grain of mustard seed was enough to plant a tree in the middle of a sea. The problem is not that we need more faith. The way to experience the

THE WAY TO EXPERIENCE THE MEASURE OF FAITH THAT CHANGES OUR BEHAVIOR IS NOT TO ASK FOR MORE FAITH, BUT RATHER TO ASK GOD FOR HELP IN YIELDING TO THE FAITH THAT IS ALREADY WITHIN US.

measure of faith that changes our behavior is not to ask for more faith, but rather to ask God for help in yielding to the faith that is already within us.

In looking at the responses that are the fruit of the Holy Spirit, do you consider some of them impossible for you to manifest in your life? Do you consider them to be such unlikely choices given the realities of adversity to the point that you even reject these truths? Have you been focused on knowing about God rather than on *knowing* God?

If you answered "yes" to any of these questions, you are being driven by your soul and trying to be like God in your own power. You are using the acquisition of information to justify the failure of your personal relation with God. Reject those thoughts, desires, and feelings of doubt, and have faith in God.

Remember that the Holy Spirit took up residence within you when you were saved. Realize that your faith offers you great power, not in yourself but from God. This power is not because you know *about* Him, but because you know Him. Daniel 11:32 says, "the people **that do know their God** shall be strong, and do exploits."

Your personal relation with God is developed as you yield to the fruit of the Spirit—Faith. You will then be conforming to His image by allowing the Holy Spirit to do the transforming. However if you focus on developing your own righteousness by acquiring information, you will yield to the work of the flesh—Doubt. This leads to conforming by performing.

Performance is *never* God's design for your life; conformance is. Man performs—that is the best we can do in our own strength. God conforms—He has the power and ability to make real and lasting change. If you're performing for God, your willingness to yield to faith is weak. Ask God instead to conform you as you trust and obey Him. As the song says, "there's no other way to be happy in Jesus, but to trust and obey."

chapter eight
MEEKNESS VS. DISCORD

GOD OFFERS THE FRUIT OF THE SPIRIT—MEEKNESS

Meekness is a fruit that is easy to overlook, but is it greatly appreciated when it is applied. Most people probably do not even recognize this fruit unless they realize the thought processes of the person who is yielding to it. You see, meekness is a fruit that is applied when someone is trying to assist a person who is actively engaged in a work of the flesh. That's why it is such a difficult fruit to yield to.

I have read that when the translators of our English Bible came to the Greek word *praotes* (meekness), they had a difficult time agreeing on a word that adequately conveyed its meaning. At first, they considered the word weakness, but that is far from accurately capturing the meaning of the word. The true meaning relates to the practice of adding saliva to help get a firm grip on something. In the days before batting gloves, baseball players would sometimes spit on their hands to get a better grip on the bat. The idea is "to add a lubricant in order to reduce friction."

What connection does that have with Christian character? In practice, meekness means "the ability for God's people to negotiate among others without causing friction." Where is *that* in our churches today? When God's people respond to each other and to a lost world in a spirit of meekness, it is sure to produce a level of respect and curiosity.

As I mentioned earlier, when I struggle with yielding to a particular fruit, I try to find people who seem to be stronger in yielding to it. I look for someone who exhibits that fruit with apparent ease. I try to learn from them how they attained the grace and faith necessary to become so successful in yielding to that particular fruit.

At a certain point in my secular career, I was promoted to the position of General Manager at my job. It was the first time I had the privilege of managing others since I had rededicated my life to the Lord. In that management position, I quickly found out that meekness would be an excellent fruit to master! Unfortunately, yielding to this fruit was a mystery to me.

However, my employer and mentor, Dan Arnold, who even now is one of my teachers and counselors, excelled in exhibiting this fruit. He is simply the meekest man I have ever met. Dan knows the value of people. He knows that while they have weaknesses, they also have strengths that offset those weaknesses. He realizes that if his organization is to benefit from those strengths, he will have to overlook some weaknesses. This is especially true in the area of personality flaws.

Most importantly, he recognizes the importance of getting a person's co-workers to overlook those weaknesses as well. He once told me there are three things working against **SATAN ALWAYS SEEKS TO GET US TO REACT TO THE WEAKNESSES OF OTHERS IMPROPERLY.** interpersonal relationships: the person's own weaknesses, the other person's weaknesses, and Satan. Satan always seeks to get us to react to the weaknesses of others improperly. In other words, there is very little chance that people will just naturally get along.

These relationships require a spiritual man or woman to add a lubricant to help reduce the friction. Dan realized the value of helping people get along with one another for the sake of keeping the "working family" together. His organization is very much like a family, and he is truly loyal to his people. He does not want to see them leave the organization, especially over personality weaknesses that could be improved with time.

He once told me that the key to running a successful organization is to "develop people daily." I have that slogan on a tab on my planner, and I move that tab forward every day. The goal is always to utilize people's strengths, but not stop there. We also need to work diligently to help them overcome their weaknesses.

However when I started working for him, his ways were not my ways. When I saw a weakness in someone, I would "share" it with them. I would give them flack for it as part of the process of "encouraging" them to shape up! I actually created more controversy with my responses than their weakness created. I caused a *lot* of friction with my leadership style, but it was the only style I knew.

So I began watching Dan, and I saw a very different type of "people development" going on. I would observe him as he discussed something with someone who was frustrated by another staff member. He would never criticize the weaker employee to the person who was complaining. Instead he would try to explain why the person may have behaved the way he did. He encouraged the complaining employee to be patient and overlook the mistake.

Then in a day or two, he would work with the person who had the weakness. He would not deride him or tell him how much trouble he was causing. Rather, he started by complimenting him on his areas of strength. Then Dan would give the person work assignments that were well thought out and designed to expose the employee's weakness to himself. Dan would work with them to encourage and advise them in the task.

In addition, he would also point out to the weaker employee things that were strengths in the life of the person who complained. This type of leadership produces a wonderful spirit of "people development" in the workplace. It took me a long time to even understand what Dan was doing. Only recently was I able to define it (much less put it into practice!) as a system of "people development."

Some people might describe Dan Arnold as a flat-liner. It seems like nothing gets him too excited. He never seems to be emotionally up or down, no matter what type of people failure he's facing. His life demonstrates the fruit of the Spirit—Meekness as he works to overcome the three enemies of relationships we talked about earlier.

What is true in the workplace is true in the body of Christ as well as in our homes. Meekness provides the necessary lubricant to help us get along with each other. You see, the burden lies with us to get along with *all* people—no matter what failings or weaknesses they have. How else can we demonstrate the love of God in the face of affliction?

"Brethren, if a man be overtaken in a fault, ye which are spiritual, restore such an one in the spirit of meekness, considering thyself, lest thou also be tempted. Bear ye one another's burdens, and so fulfil the law of Christ. For if a man think himself to be something, when he is nothing, he deceiveth himself." Galatians 6:1-3

We have a biblically-mandated role to play when faced with weakness on the part of a fellow believer. The purpose is not to condemn or judge, it is to restore him to his former standing in fellowship with Christ. The tool for this task is the spirit of meekness. Whenever we come in contact with a person's weakness, we should begin a healing and restoration process.

What Paul is telling us here is that when someone steps forward with a fault, we should restore that person in a way that doesn't cause friction! Some people want to proclaim it from the rooftops when someone falls. That is guaranteed to cause friction! If we don't extend meekness to others when they fall, then we ourselves are in danger of being overtaken. Such a fall will surely be met with the same discord that we sowed in the lives of others who needed meekness from us but failed to receive it.

God's people should always be willing to encourage others in a way that reduces friction. That means we cannot react by saying whatever we feel like, even to those with glaring personality flaws. That is anything but meekness. In fact that is the devil's alternative to meekness, the work of the flesh—Discord.

We Often Prefer the Work of the Flesh—Discord

As the leader of a ministry that produces a large number of adult converts, I have seen firsthand the damage that is done by discord. It can bring great harm, especially to the life of a baby believer. That is part of the devil's plan to keep new believers from reaching God's purpose for their lives. Many times I've heard it said that the Christian Army is the only one that shoots its own wounded. I don't want to believe that saying, but as is so often the case with clichés, there is some truth to it.

Discord is one of the most damaging works of the flesh. Webster's 1828 Dictionary defines discord as "any disagreement which produces angry passions, contest, disputes, litigation, or war." Discord may exist in any relationship. There have been problems in families ever since Cain and Abel. It is no wonder that discord is a problem in church families as well.

James, one of the Bible's best educators on human behavior, had a lot to say about the value of meekness and the danger of discord. After giving several illustrations of what great damage the tongue can do (including comparing it to a raging wildfire!), James also gave us the cure.

"Who is a wise man and endued with knowledge among you? let him shew out of a good conversation his works with meekness of wisdom. But if ye have bitter envying and strife in your hearts, glory not, and lie not against the truth. This wisdom descendeth not from above, but is earthly, sensual, devilish. For where envying and strife is, there is confusion and every evil work. But the wisdom that is from above is first pure, then peaceable, gentle, and easy to be intreated, full of mercy and good fruits, without partiality, and without hypocrisy. And the fruit of righteousness is sown in peace of them that make peace." James 3:13-18

It is the job of wise and knowledgeable teachers to teach others with meekness how to live by example. The teacher, because he has the works to back up his words, can explain to believers that being a busybody is not from God, but instead is devilish and sensual—that is it stimulates our senses and emotions. A church without such a leader will struggle with tongue troubles and experience confusion and evil work within the body.

Remember that God never causes confusion; that is the work of the devil. This passage in James describes the spirit that will permeate the church if the people invest in opportunities to make peace whenever possible. Godly leadership yields wonderful results. It is a great blessing to have a teacher in the church who can train others—someone who demonstrates the fruit of meekness.

The lessons need to include how to develop faith, grace and obedience in learning to yield to the fruit of meekness. It would save a lot of trouble in our churches. My home church, North Love Baptist Church in Rockford, Illinois is a meek church, but it was not always that way. God has used our pastor to foster such an atmosphere. God knew that we would need an environment where baby Christians would grow, and He has sent many of them our way.

REMEMBER THAT GOD NEVER CAUSES CONFUSION; THAT IS THE WORK OF THE DEVIL.

When Reformers Unanimous began in 1996, I had a student who, for the sake of privacy, I will call Joan. Joan attended class nearly every Friday for six months. She almost never missed a session. However no matter how many times my wife and I invited her to church, she would firmly but kindly say, "No thanks."

I knew she wasn't attending church anywhere else, so one week I asked why she wasn't willing to try our church. She explained to me that she did not have a dress to wear, and was waiting to get enough money to buy one. Of course I told her that she didn't have to wear a dress to attend our church. She said that she knew that, but insisted that she wanted to have something special to wear the first time she came to church.

We were impressed with her desire, so my wife and I offered to buy her a dress. She refused saying, "God wants me to buy it for myself!" I was out of ammunition so I just waited. Sure enough, about six weeks later, Joan told me she had saved enough money for a dress and would be at church the next Sunday. My wife and I were overjoyed.

That Sunday, Lori and I were eager to meet her. When we got to the top of the stairs, we saw Joan there hanging up her coat. When I saw her, my heart sank. She had purchased a very short miniskirt. I sympathetically thought, "Well, she doesn't know any better." We told her we were glad to see her, and welcomed her to the church. She sat with us in our usual place near the front of the church.

Everyone was kind to Joan as we introduced her to our friends, and no one stared or glared at her for the skirt she had chosen. But by the time the choir walked in, Joan had begun to realize that her choice of dress wasn't like the other ladies there. She tugged on the hem of her skirt, trying to bring it closer to her knees. She was uncomfortable, but she was learning and observing. The most important thing is that her heart was in the right place.

After the service, however, things went downhill fast. As I was talking to someone else, Joan was approached by one of the pillars of the church. This wonderful woman proceeded to inform Joan that her clothing was inappropriate. She complained that her husband "could not keep his eyes off your nakedness" during the service. She chided Joan for her indecency and rebellion in the house of God.

Joan fled the church building in tears. She has never been back to either church or class since. Indeed, several situations like this happened in the early days of the RU ministry. In hindsight, it was a necessary period of growth in our churches history. It was a challenging time. Those lessons we learned in the church reinforced the lesson I learned from Dan Arnold about the vital importance of the fruit of the Spirit—Meekness.

To be effective in work and ministry, I had to learn to submit to the Holy Spirit's direction and work to reduce friction between people. When I told Pastor Kingsbury about Joan's experience, he was heartbroken. He immediately began preaching and teaching on the importance of meekness. Drawing from Scripture and the lessons he had learned about taming the tongue, he showed our congregation how to yield to meekness.

Within a short time, the very spirit and atmosphere of North Love Baptist Church changed. It became fertile soil for baby Christians to grow. There they could reach levels of maturity beyond what might be possible in most churches. Why? Because a wise man, our pastor, used his knowledge to show others how it ought to be done.

If we are going to destroy discord, we must learn to restrain our tongues. We must yield to the Spirit's leading to reduce friction between others. And finally, we must take what we have learned and teach it to others. As Dan Arnold taught me, work to develop people daily.

chapter nine

TEMPERANCE VS. SELF-INDULGENCE

SOME PEOPLE THINK THAT TEMPERANCE SHOULD BE FIRST ON THE LIST OF THE FRUIT OF THE SPIRIT TO WHICH WE MUST YIELD. But Paul listed it last, under the direction of the Holy Spirit—not because it is the least of the fruits, but rather because it is the completion of them. It takes temperance to put us into a position of being Spirit-led believers.

Temperance is essential to keep the passions of the mind, will and emotions suppressed, allowing the Holy Spirit to rule our lives. But when questioned about temperance, many people describe it as self-control. Even some of the songs our children learn in Sunday school talk about the importance of self-control. Nothing could be further from the truth!

As we have seen throughout this book, we ought never to be in control of ourselves. In reality, self-control is an oxymoron. There is nothing about me that I can control that will gain God's approval and acceptance. To succeed in the Christian life, I must stop trying to control myself. The more I control myself, the less God is in control of me. Thus the fruit of the Spirit—Temperance properly understood is Spirit-control, or more specifically, "Spirit-control in all of life's pleasures."

God Offers the Fruit of the Spirit—Temperance

Life, as given by God, offers many pleasures. However the devil seeks to take those pleasures and turn them into objects of lust. His goal is to get us to enjoy God's pleasures, but in a selfish way, creating appetites that are ungodly and out of control. The absence of Spirit-control is the single most fleshly action that produces habitual sins.

To fully enjoy the benefits of the pleasures God offers, we must yield to the fruit of the Spirit—Temperance. Many Christians fail to cultivate this fruit, opting rather to reject most of life's pleasures in an attempt to control the temptation that fuels fleshly lusts. I believe this leads God's people into a spiritual bondage, often called legalism. Many people are confused about legalism.

There is a legalism that is based on earning our way to Heaven based on our good works. This is legalistic justification. True Christians understand that this is false. Yet many settle into a legalistic sanctification, whereby we strive to obtain a level of righteousness in our own power. This leads to self-righteousness. So people who readily accepted justification as God doing all of the work approach sanctification as if they must paddle their own canoe. We believe we need to help God out!

This is a mistake in Christian development that derails most Christians from experiencing the abundant Christian life. Although we may avoid the obviously unrighteous sins listed in Galatians 5:19-21, we still find ourselves indulging in the natural affections of our "good flesh." This leads to discouragement and frustration in the Christian life, *as we try hard to do better*, but continually fail.

We serve until we're half-dead, but receive little joy in return. So the mind, will and emotions begin to tell us that our lack of joy is due to not acting righteously enough. Further they say that failure is because we are allowing ourselves to enjoy too many of life's pleasures. To compensate, we reject all forms of enjoyment to try to please God, much as a monk

SO PEOPLE WHO READILY ACCEPTED JUSTIFICATION AS GOD DOING ALL OF THE WORK APPROACH SANCTIFICATION AS IF THEY MUST PADDLE THEIR OWN CANOE.

tries to gain God's favor through abstinence. This is a perversion of God's designed intention of pleasure.

Admittedly we should avoid situations that could lead us to compromise our Christian walk. Nevertheless, we must be willing to allow God to put us into circumstances that will permit us to yield to the fruit of temperance. It is neither possible nor desirable to totally isolate ourselves from the world. When the Spirit produces temperance, God is in control of the pleasures of life, and His Spirit directs our enjoyment of them.

I know some people who refuse to own a television set. They will not eat any food that might be nutritionally weak. They will not go to a fireworks show in the city square on Independence Day. They hide in their basements with the lights out on Halloween. They don't let their kids play organized sports. They don't go to the mall. They rip pages out of their magazines. They do all this and more to try to prevent themselves or those they care about from being tempted.

Now before you start thinking that I feel it is acceptable to carelessly place yourself or those you love in harm's way, please notice the context of my statements. This entire book proves that I am a strong proponent of avoiding the snares of the devil. However, sometimes it is God's plan for us to endure temptation. It is His design.

Remember after Jesus' baptism how he went into the desert and fasted for forty days? The Bible says He was led there *by the Spirit* to be tempted by the devil. (Matt. 14) It was God's plan. In teaching us how to pray, Jesus said we ought to ask "lead us not into temptation." Why would such a request even exist if God were not in control of whether or not we go through temptation?

To be sure, God wants to develop our souls to yield to the inner man's leading of temperance. God wants us to be under His control in the pleasurable circumstances of life as well as the unpleasurable ones. The only way to avoid temptation completely is to sever your relationship with the outside world. And there are some denominations that suggest just that.

However we cannot do that and still function in society, much less be effective in evangelism. The devil tries to get us to give up all interaction with the pleasures of life and *do good in our own power.* Then, as we are performing instead of transforming, he will place an incredibly appealing temptation in our way. In our own power, we will not be able to overcome and sustain victory.

We will eventually indulge in our fleshly desire, because it is impossible to endure temptations from the devil indefinitely in our own power. As I write this, we have just witnessed the incredible devastation from Hurricane Katrina on New Orleans, Louisiana. The city, most of which sits below sea level, is protected by a system of levees to keep out the water. During the flooding following that massive storm, the levees held out for a while, but eventually two of them broke, flooding much of the city with water. You may hold out for a while on your own, but eventually, you will fall. Your self-imposed walls are no match for the incredible pressures of Satan without the power of God to protect you from the storms of life.

Being laden with hidden desires and secret sins that make us feel dirty and defeated is spiritual bondage. But that is what happens when the soul of man controls the spirit of man. Ironically, this is the end result of the self-control that so many people promote—bondage!

God has a better way. His plan is for us to face temptation with the confidence that He has provided a way of escape. That way of escape is revealed to us by the inner man. God, communicating with our spirit through His Spirit will enable us to walk away from a pleasure temporarily or abstain from it all together.

When we allow this type of spiritual interaction to take place, we are exercising our faith. It will grow and strengthen, just like a muscle does when exercised. This is spiritual growth and development. It occurs when we give every good and bad thing to God, staying under His control in all things.

Let's revisit Romans 6 again and see how it explains God's demands for abstinence from sinful behavior. As a result of God's work on our behalf, sin should be decreasing in our lives, not increasing. "What shall we say then? Shall we continue in sin, that grace may about? God forbid. How shall we, that are dead to sin, live any longer therein?" (Rom. 6:1-2)

God destroyed the power that sin had over us so that we could serve something other than ourselves. This Someone that we now serve (through submission to His leading) brings us freedom. "Knowing this, that our old man is crucified with him, that the body of sin might be destroyed, that henceforth we should not serve sin. For he that is dead is free from sin." (Rom. 6:6-7)

God does not want us to yield to those old desires anymore. The power is gone, but the desire is still there. According to Romans 6:12-14, to destroy the desire we must yield to God's power in our life.

"Let not sin therefore reign in your mortal body, that ye should obey it in the lusts thereof. Neither yield ye your members (body parts) as instruments of unrighteousness unto sin: but yield yourselves unto God, as those that are alive from the dead, and your members (body parts) as instruments of righteousness unto God. For sin shall not have dominion (power) over you: for ye are not under the law (when man does the work), but under grace." Romans 6:12-14

If we indulge fleshly appetites, they will grow stronger. If we feed our Spirit-led appetites, they will grow stronger as well. God will never feed a fleshly appetite, but we will—after we tire of performing in our own power.

"Know ye not, that to whom ye yield yourselves servants to obey, his servant ye are to whom ye obey; whether of sin unto death, or of obedience unto righteousness? Being then made free form sin, ye became the servants of righteousness." Romans 6:16, 18

So we could never justify willfully placing ourselves in harm's way, making it harder for us to avoid sin. Certainly God is against feeding our sinful appetites. But we equally need to be on guard against placing ourselves in a position conducive to developing the outer man's self-righteousness. That form of development hinders God's work on our behalf.

Friend, our Heavenly Father will rip the cover right off of your self-righteous behavior. I would hate to see what He will permit you to endure in your own power. That is a very hard way to learn this lesson in your life. "Whom the Lord loveth, he chasteneth." (Heb. 12:6)

Rather than utterly rejecting what may be a new view of self-control to you in regards to life's pleasures, please consider this: If we try to control life's pleasures, then life's pleasures will eventually control us. But if God controls our pleasures, we will be safe from harm in the face of temptation, because His plan for us always includes a way of escape.

We Often Prefer the Work of the Flesh—Self-Indulgence

The reason that soul-control (what most people call self-control) is often taught in churches is because of spiritual weakness. It takes strong, exercised faith to yield to the fruit of the Spirit—Temperance rather than engaging in the work of the flesh—Self-Indulgence. But that creates a vicious cycle. To offset our spiritual weakness, we try harder to learn how to control ourselves.

That is, we reject God's control of our lives, and fall back on our own control instead to keep from doing wrong. But when we try to control ourselves, it is just the flesh trying to control the flesh. Good flesh is just as bad as bad flesh. The ultimate end of this cycle is self-indulgence. Self-indulgence is when "self-control ceases to control itself."

We lose the battles of spiritual warfare when we indulge our bad appetites. This hinders our spiritual walk. To help illustrate the difference between temperance and self-indulgence, let's look at three different kinds of appetites. These appetites are the determining factor in every decision that we make—good or bad.

Some appetites need to be satisfied. These are good appetites. In our fallen condition, most people do not naturally have appetites for things that are good. Set an apple and a piece of cake on the counter and see which one a child will pick (or an adult for that matter)! To gain good appetites, we must determine what creates those appetites and then feed them. As a result of feeding them, they will be temporarily satisfied. It is good for them to be satisfied, and it is also good for them not to be permanently satisfied.

You see, if our appetites remained satisfied, we would never need to feed them again. As a result, we would lose our appetites for that which is good. Again, the temporary satisfaction that comes from feeding a good appetite causes it to grow. As it grows, it needs to be fed again. Good appetites should neither be overfed nor starved. They should instead be fed on a regularly scheduled basis.

Some examples of good appetites that need to be created and fed are a daily "God and I" time, church attendance, serving, soul winning, family time, work ethics, nutritional food, physical exercise, etc. Matthew 5:6 says, "Blessed are they which do hunger and thirst after righteousness: for they shall be filled." This verse tells us that God will completely provide for our yearning to yield to the inner man (i.e., righteousness). Obviously, these are appetites that must be regularly fed or else the cares of this world will eventually draw us dry. However, Jesus assures us that whenever we seek to be filled with the Spirit's leading, we will always be fed by God. Such appetites will lead us to even greater blessings.

Some appetites need to be starved. There are appetites that are sinful that should never be fed at any time. These appetites can very quickly grow with just the slightest bit of feeding. All they require is a look, a thought, a point or a click—if we indulge these appetites, they will soon control us. These appetites are never fully satisfied; they always require more feeding. Their desire to be fed brings a nagging misery as they attack our minds.

Some of these appetites are outward works of the flesh such as drugs, alcohol, gambling, pornography, anger or pride. Others are the inward works of the flesh we've been studying—self-love, frustration, worry, etc. These behaviors must be strictly avoided. You must through God's strength develop your inner man to reject these insatiable appetites of the soul. If you do not, they will destroy your life sooner rather than later.

"All the labour of man is for his mouth, and yet the appetite is not filled. Better is the sight of the eyes than the wandering of his desire: this is also vanity and vexation of spirit." Ecclesiastes 6:7, 9

"He that loveth silver shall not be satisfied with silver; nor he that loveth abundance with increase: this is also vanity. When good increase, they are increased that eat them: and what good is there to the owners thereof, saving the beholding of them with their eyes?" Ecclesiastes 5:10-11

"And have no fellowship with the unfruitful works of darkness, but rather reprove them. For it is a shame even to speak of those things which are done of them in secret." Ephesians 5:11-12

These verses remind us that all of our efforts to satisfy our wrong desires will be to no avail. Whether we get what our appetite desires or whether it is withheld from us, we will not be satisfied either way.

Some appetites need to be suppressed. These are appetites for things for which God gave us a natural need, drive, or use for. They are intended for our good pleasure, but when indulged with abandon will lead to lusts which control us. These appetites for things that are good but potentially dangerous must be controlled as we yield to the fruit of the Spirit—Temperance.

Abuse of these appetites will probably not destroy your life sooner, but if they are fed without temperance, they will destroy your life later. Remember that these appetites are not sinful. God gave them to us. Many of them are necessary for us to live, yet they can still lead us into bondage is we are not careful. Some of these appetites are food, sleep, relaxations, money, sexual relations with your spouse, work, play, and entertainment.

In I Corinthians 6:12, Paul talked about these appetites. "All things are lawful unto me, but all things are not expedient: all things are lawful for me, but I will not be brought under the power of any." He realized the importance of controlling good appetites, and was

WHETHER WE GET WHAT OUR APPETITE DESIRES OR WHETHER IT IS WITHHELD FROM US, WE WILL NOT BE SATISFIED EITHER WAY.

careful to do so. He did not feed appetites that were not beneficial. He starved appetites that would be considered fleshly. He did this because he refused to be the servant of anything other than the Spirit of God.

Control over these appetites will require an effort on our part. This effort is not to do the work ourselves; rather it is an effort to allow God to do the work for us. Temperance is being under the control of the Holy Spirit. Appetite control requires putting off the old man and putting on the new. "But put ye on the Lord Jesus Christ, and make not provision for the flesh, to fulfil the lusts thereof." (Rom. 13:14)

CONCLUSION

THE WORDS THAT PAUL WROTE IN GALATIANS 5 JUST BEFORE AND JUST AFTER LISTING THE WORKS OF THE FLESH AND THE FRUIT OF THE SPIRIT BRING THIS ENTIRE STUDY OF THE ABUNDANT CHRISTIAN LIFE TOGETHER. Verse 16 says, "This I say then, Walk in the Spirit, and ye shall not fulfil the lust of the flesh." Verse 23 says of the fruit of the Spirit, "Against such there is no law."

To be Spirit-led believers, we simply must take repeated steps "in the Spirit." Though we will occasionally reject or overlook the Spirit's leading and may actually fulfill a lust of the flesh, we should not need a law of God or man to get us back in line. The God who saved us and the God who changes us is also the God who keeps us. He is able to keep us from falling—if we let Him. To paraphrase what Paul said, "If you will simply abide in Christ, God will do all the work for you.

I would like to add one final thought concerning the nine fruits of the Spirit. In the Gospels, Christ summed up the Old Testament and the Law with two basic commandments. They were to love God and to love others. *All* the Law and the commandments hung on these two commands, both of which are to LOVE!

Many Christians, for the sake of judging others (or to at least avoid the self-sacrifice of offering mercy to them), have rejected the verse that tells us that God is love. They prefer to remind us all that God is judgment, and God is righteous, and God is jealous, and God is holy; and He is! But a brief study of Scripture will show that the attribute God and His Son Jesus used when painting their self-portraits was LOVE.

If you were to ask me, "How can I develop my inner man to the point where I am abiding in Christ effectively enough to act and respond under the influence of the nine fruits of the Spirit?" I would suggest the following commitments on your part:

- Pray every day that God will allow circumstances in your life that will break your outer man.
- Pray that those circumstances will cause you to yield to the inner man, allowing God's light to shine through that hole in your soul.
- Cultivate a heart for knowing God by developing your relationship with Him early every day. (Don't eat until you have prayed; don't sleep unless you have meditated on the Bible. Feed no physical appetite until your spiritual appetite is satisfied.)
- When you become aware of someone with a need, ask the Spirit how you should respond. If you are led to give, always respond with the fruit of the Spirit—love. Give of yourself willingly, without any thought of return.

If you will yield to love, then more often than not, the other fruits will fall in line and become easier to yield to as well. Why? Because the greatest of these is LOVE. (I Cor. 13:13)

In the final section of this book, we will explain how God has used certain techniques that He has shown me over the years to develop my inner man. You see, to die daily is simply to reject pleasing your soul in exchange for pleasing your spirit. As you do this, the outer man will be destroyed and the inner man will be developed.

But before we go on, let's stop and look one more time at the righteous actions and reactions of the fruit of the Spirit beside the self-righteous actions and reactions of the works of the flesh. Looking at the definitions of these 18 actions and reactions, you will be able to determine, based on your responses, if you are walking "in the Spirit" or "after the flesh." You will know if you are doing God's will in His power, or doing good will in your own power. Place a checkmark in the box (❑) that describes your strength or weakness in a particular fruit. Most Christians struggle with at least three. Which ones do you struggle to yield to? This will give you a better idea of the areas you need to work on.

The Fruits of the Spirit and the Works of the Flesh
Self-Evaluation

When I am faced with an opportunity to serve, I exhibit:
- ❏ **Love:** the willing, sacrificial giving of oneself for the benefit of others without thought of return
- ❏ **Self-Love:** the willing or unwilling giving of oneself to benefit others with selfish thoughts of return

When faced with a "whammy," I exhibit:
- ❏ **Joy:** a cheerful, calm delight in all the circumstances of life
- ❏ **Frustration:** a rejection or unhappy refusal in life's circumstances

When I experience things that seem to be harmful, I exhibit:
- ❏ **Peace:** to be safe from harm in spirit, mind and body
- ❏ **Worry:** to live in fear of harm in spirit, mind and body

When people fall short of my expectations for them, I exhibit:
- ❏ **Longsuffering:** an enduring temperament that expresses itself in patience with the shortcomings of others
- ❏ **Quick-Tempered:** irritability that negatively excites the passions

When people are inconsiderate to me or to things important to me, I exhibit:
- ❏ **Gentleness:** softness in manners
- ❏ **Harshness:** roughness in manners, temper or words

When I see a need in someone's life, I exhibit:
- ❏ **Goodness:** conforming our lives and conversations to behave benevolently toward others
- ❏ **Meanness:** refusing to be liberal with charity, thus avoiding any personal expense

When I am challenged in my beliefs, I exhibit:
- ❏ **Faith:** a personal measurement of the level of confidence in what Christ has done and will do in, through and for us
- ❏ **Doubt:** an attitude of unbelief, characterized by rebellion and disobedience toward God

When someone is causing trouble or complaining about others, I exhibit:
- ☐ **Meekness:** the ability for God's people to negotiate among others without causing friction
- ☐ **Discord:** any disagreement which produces angry passions, contests, disputes, litigation, or war

When something tries to control my mind, will, or emotions, I exhibit:
- ☐ **Temperance:** Spirit-controlled in all of life's pleasure
- ☐ **Self-Indulgence:** when self-control ceases to control itself

List your struggles and weaknesses:

Fruit Strengths:	Flesh Weaknesses:
_____	_____
_____	_____
_____	_____
_____	_____
_____	_____
_____	_____
_____	_____

As you develop your relationship with the Lord, ask Him to give you the strength to yield to the Spirit in your areas of weakness. You may consider looking at this chart or something similar every 90 days as your relationship develops.

SECTION THREE

THE EXCHANGED LIFE:

Exchanging Redundant Life for Abundant Life

INTRODUCTION

IN SECTION TWO, WE DESCRIBED MAN TRYING TO ACT LIKE GOD IN HIS OWN POWER AS BEING SELF-RIGHTEOUS. Did you see some of your behaviors listed? I know that when God first revealed my self-righteous flesh to me, I was amazed at how carnal my Christian efforts had become. It was extremely convicting. But the question is, how do you know when you are responding in the Spirit or in the soul; righteously rather than self-righteously? How can we notice our flesh and immediately correct it, or better still, how can we develop spiritually to the point where we avoid fleshly responses? How can we exchange fleshly behavior for following the Spirit's promptings in response to life's problems?

Well, the answer is not going to be found in the depth of your knowledge about God. Rather it comes in the depth of your personal relation with God. You see, God has created a means by which we can determine (rather quickly) whether we are putting forth our own effort to perform or whether His Spirit is leading as we transform. The answer is found in how we navigate His Word.

Christ revealed Himself to mankind in two forms: as the incarnate Son of God, and as the transcribed Word of God. John 1:14 says, "And the Word was made flesh, and dwelt among us, (and we beheld his glory, the glory as of the only begotten of the Father) full of grace and truth." God has given us His Word as a form of communication with our spirit, through His indwelling Holy Spirit.

The author of the book of Hebrews said, "There remaineth therefore a rest to the people of God." (Heb. 4:9) He was describing the covenant relationship with God we can have through His Son

Jesus. This relationship allows us to rest while Christ does the work in our life. He goes on to say, "For he that is entered into his rest, he also hath ceased from his own works, as God did from his." (Heb. 4:10)

This is simply reminding us that, just as the work of God in creation is complete, so too is the work of Christ in redemption. They have ceased from their works; and we to can cease from our *trying hard to do better*. We have a different and better responsibility now—we are to work to enter into God's rest. "Let us labour therefore to enter into that rest." (Heb. 4:11a) We are offered a rest *in* Christ here on earth to be followed by a rest *with* Christ in eternity!

The writer follows these encouraging words by telling us how to keep from hindering God's work on our behalf. Hebrews 4:12 says, "For the word of God is quick, and powerful, and sharper than any twoedged sword, piercing even to the dividing asunder of soul and spirit, and of the joints and marrow, and is a discerner of the thoughts and intents of the heart." I believe this verse teaches us exactly how to determine if we are engaged in righteous or self-righteous behavior.

Simply put, we see here how the transcribed Son of God (the Bible) provides benefits to us through the indwelling Spirit of God. This verse is often memorized and quoted, but it is seldom fully understood as to its proper meaning. Let's dissect and define the parts of this verse so that we have a better understanding of what God is trying to teach us about the Bible

The Word of God: the Bible
[the Bible] is quick: alive
and powerful: able to produce
dividing asunder: separating into parts
of soul: your mind, will and emotions
and spirit: God's mind, will and emotions
of the joints: outer bone parts
and marrow: inner bone parts
a discerner: discover through observation
thoughts: meditations
intents: focus
of the heart: your trigger

This verse tells us that the Word of God has much in common with the Spirit of God. They are both alive and powerful! And consider this truth: it's like a sword that separates the soul and the spirit into two parts. Why is this important? Because, as we saw in Section Two, your soul will try to act like your spirit. The two will begin to coagulate.

Without a proper application of the Word, you will not be able to determine whether your soul is doing the work (self-righteousness) or your spirit is allowing God to do the work (righteousness). I believe the reference to joints and marrow is simply an illustration of the same truth—separating the outer man (soul) from the inner man (spirit).

You can be sure that if you will use the Bible properly, not only will it keep your soul from trying to act like God in its own power, but it will reveal to you, through personal observation of your heart, what your true meditation and focus in life really is. The Spirit of God will reveal those truths to you in your inner man. This will either lead to confirmation that you are doing right, or conviction that you need to change.

Remember that your heart is the trigger. We will discuss this truth in detail in this section, but the heart is the trigger between the soul and the spirit. It can be affected by all three parts of your soul as well as by all three parts of your spirit. Your heart can think with your mind or with the mind of Christ. It can focus on the will of man or on the will of God.

If your trigger is metaphorically tripped in the direction of your spirit, you will think, feel and want the things of God. If your heart is tripped in the direction of your soul, you will think, feel and want the things of this world. It is very encouraging to realize that God will use His Word to discern your trigger position and reveal it to you in the inner man. YET PEOPLE SAY THEY DON'T HAVE TIME TO SPEND A FEW MINUTES IN THE WORD EVERY DAY!

Now let's conclude this introduction with a brief explanation of the three-fold role of the inner man. This will help you realize the potential damage to your intimacy with Christ when we fail to use the Word to discern our trigger position that the Word may divide our soul and spirit asunder. The inner man, where your spirit dwells along with the Spirit of God, is the birthplace of three major communications with God: intuition, worship and conscience.

Intuition is God's personal leading in your life. In John 16:14, we are told the Comforter will be the Spirit of Jesus (Truth) and that "he (the Spirit) shall receive of mine (Jesus'), and shall shew it unto you." That indicates a personal revelation from the Son of God through the Spirit of God to the child of God.

Realizing that Jesus is the only mediator between God and man, we see again that our inner man is a "Walkie/Talkie" for God. God communicates to our Intercessor His direction and leading for our life. Christ then communicates that to the indwelling Holy Spirit. Finally, the Spirit passes on the communication to our spirit. If our trigger (heart) is in the right position, we will head in the direction He leads, thus following God's divine plan.

But if there is a wrong focus (intent) or improper meditation (thoughts) in our soul, then we will weaken the communication link between our spirit and God's Spirit. Proper focus and positive meditation will strengthen that intuitive communication from God. Obviously improper focus or negative meditation will weaken the intuitive communication from Him.

Worship is the way in which we express our love toward God (and He toward us). This too takes place in the inner man as a communication between our spirit and God's Spirit. Our communications are sent Heavenward, and assimilated through Christ. Jesus said, "God is a Spirit, and they that worship him must worship him in spirit and in truth." (John 4:24) This very clearly delineates a role for both the Spirit and the Truth (Christ) in our worship of God.

There cannot be communication between different natures. The soul cannot worship God. It would not if it could; the soul only worships self. Thus the unsaved man who does not possess a living spirit, and the saved man who will not use his spirit to worship God are equally unqualified to enjoy fellowship with God. If you struggle to understand or accept this truth, let the Word reveal it to you in your inner man.

"But as it is written, Eye hath not seen, nor ear heard, neither have entered into the heart of man, the things which God hath prepared for them that love him. <u>But God hath revealed them unto us by his Spirit</u>; for the Spirit searcheth all things, yea, the deep things of God. <u>For what man knoweth the things of a man, save the spirit of man which is in him?</u> even so the things of God knoweth no man, but the Spirit of God. Now we have received, not the spirit of the world, but the spirit which is of God; that <u>we might know the things that are freely given to us of God</u>." I Corinthians 2:9-12

If our trigger (heart) is in the right position, we will worship God and enjoy sweet fellowship with Him. However if it is not, then our worship will be dry, uneventful and show a spirit of ingratitude toward

God and apathy toward His goals for our lives.

Conscience is the third form of communication that takes place in the inner man. This one is probably the most confusing to people. The conscience functions both in the life of the believer, and in the life of a lost man who is an unregenerate dichotomy (containing a dead spirit). The primary function of the conscience is to correct us and render us uneasy when we violate God's plan for our daily lives. We frequently refer to this process as conviction.

This form of communication is absolutely vital to the other two. If you reject the voice of conscience, then you will weaken the intuition and hinder your worship. A violated conscience places an offense between you and God. When God communicates to your conscience in your inner man, it is done by His Spirit. He reproves you

SINCE THE CONSCIENCE OF A SINNER DOES NOT EMBRACE THE LIFE OF GOD IT IS ACCOUNTED DEAD, THOUGH IT MAY APPEAR TO BE ACTIVE ACCORDING TO MAN'S FEELING.

of sin, or confirms that you are under the His control (righteousness). This is what Jesus said He would do for us. (John 16:8)

Having an active conscience does not mean that a person is a regenerated believer. We know that God allows the conscience of a dead spirit to operate within a man in order to bring him to the realization that he is a sinner in need of a Savior. In the Garden of Eden, Adam's spirit had died, but his conscience was still active. That is what caused him to avoid God and try to do good in his own power (making aprons of fig leaves).

This is not to say that an active conscience is alive. Biblically speaking to be alive, you must possess the life of God. An unregenerate spirit is dead and without the life of God. Watchman Nee once wrote, "Anything void of God's life is considered dead. Since the conscience of a sinner does not embrace the life of God it is accounted dead, though it may appear to be active according to man's feeling. Such activity of the conscience augments the anguish of a sinner. In initiating His work of salvation, the first step of the Holy Spirit is to awaken this comatose conscience."

When man is regenerated and his spirit comes alive, this third form of communication becomes a powerful tool to keep him in a right relationship with God. If you will obey the voice of conscience, immediately confessing and rejecting whatever violation against God that it reveals, through that obedience the quality of your intuition (leading) and worship (fellowship) will increase.

If you reject this form of communication through neglect or outright disobedience, you hinder God's leading and restrict your worship of Him. Once again, I remind you, that the decision to follow the conscience is found in the position of the trigger that is the heart. Is it angled in the direction of the spirit or the soul?

In this final section, chapters 1-4 will show you how to properly use the Bible to discern the trigger position of your heart. Chapters 5-9 will show you how to maintain your heart to ensure it remains in the proper position. As you begin to develop these two spiritual truths, (discerning your heart's position and making necessary adjustments) you will find your life filled with all the fullness of God.

The key verses for this final section are found in Ephesians 3:14-19.

"For this cause I…would grant you, according to the riches of his glory, to be <u>strengthened</u> with might <u>by his Spirit in the inner man</u>; That <u>Christ may dwell in your hearts by faith</u>; that ye, being rooted and grounded in love, May be able to comprehend with all saints what is the breadth, and length, and depth, and height; And to know the love of Christ, which passeth knowledge, that ye <u>might be filled with all the fulness of God</u>."

This passage teaches us that we can be filled with all the fullness of God if "Christ will dwell in our heart by faith." This dwelling of Christ within the heart takes place as we are strengthened by His Spirit in the inner man through faith. We will discuss how to use the Bible to lead your heart to dwell on Christ. And we'll look at how to increase your faith in order to keep it there. Those are the requirements to be filled with God. It is the conclusion of the whole matter!

chapter one

READING YOUR BIBLE —INFORMATIONAL

"THAT THE GOD OF OUR LORD JESUS CHRIST, THE FATHER OF GLORY, MAY GIVE UNTO YOU THE SPIRIT OF WISDOM AND REVELATION IN THE KNOWLEDGE OF HIM:" EPHESIANS 1:17

If you have not read the introduction to this section, please do not start reading this chapter. Instead, go back and read it, possibly more than once, to ensure you understand the truths it presents. They are integral to your understanding the final part of this book. If you did read the introduction, you know that we are going to look at how to use your Bible to separate your soul and spirit to discern your heart's trigger position. You will learn how to dwell on Christ rather than on the things of the world.

How does reading the Bible help you dwell on Christ in your heart? Well, to be honest, it's only a small part. You might describe it as a first step. Reading your Bible will not help you to dwell on Christ after you close the book, unless you follow the step of reading with the next three steps we'll look at.

This chapter is not a "bash you till you read your Bible" chapter. Rather, I will attempt to show you why you may not enjoy reading and may struggle with having a personal time each day to read the Bible. You may also learn why, even when you read your Bible regularly, you may feel like it is doing little for your personal relation with God.

I have heard people say, "It is unfortunate, but to many, the Bible is God's unopened love letter." I don't think that's accurate. Most Christians open their Bibles and read them. They start reading, but they quit. Preachers often try to get their members to commit to a daily Bible reading schedule. Yet that doesn't work for most people.

Even if they continue to read their Bibles, it seldom helps. Most people who quit reading their Bible do so because it hasn't significantly helped their walk with God. They may have read their Bible regularly in the hope that it would help, but still see little growth in their personal relation with the Author. The primary reason that Bible reading does little for a Christian's walk is that it is not *relational*, but *informational*. It doesn't develop your walk with God. It increases your knowledge of God.

What the Bible describes as a "walk with God" has very little to do with paging daily through His Word. That is only a start, not an end. Reading the Bible is a means to the end. The phrase "walk with God" is similar in meaning to the word "disciple." The word literally means a student who follows a teacher.

This concept is what the Bible means when it says, "Walk in the Spirit, and ye shall not fulfil the lusts of the flesh." (Gal. 5:16) We have already seen that the lusts of the flesh are the desires of the soul to submit to the temptations of the body. Thus Paul tells us that if we walk after the influence of the Spirit of God, we will do what He wants rather than what we want.

This has been a basic truth throughout our discussion of behavioral modification. Thus reading your Bible will give you the steps to take that will lead you in the right paths. However, this will not happen with every verse or chapter that you read. This is especially true if you're *performing* through a Bible reading plan. Let me explain it this way.

How many times have you been reading your Bible, and all of a sudden you see something that you never saw before? I believe every Christian will experience this many times, if they are rejecting and confessing sin, and reading their Bibles with some regularity. Now who do you think it is that is prompting you with that Scriptural revelation? Do you think it's the devil? Well then, pray tell, by process of elimination, Who is it? It's the Spirit of God of course!

But a person who's performing can't stop reading when they see a truth. There is more Bible to read…and they're already three days behind schedule! Now this Spirit-led prompting (which we identified as intuition in the introduction) only occurs if your conscience is right with God (void of offense). Remember that intuition is God revealing His supernatural direction to your spirit through His Spirit in your inner man.

When you are reading your Bible, the Spirit of God will actually prompt you to stop and consider something. If you obey that prompting to stop your reading, you are "walking after the Spirit." Then the Spirit will begin to enlighten you as you take the next step with the Word (which we'll discuss in chapter 2). This Spirit-led enlightenment is God showing you something that you will need to get through your tough day. Obedience to this prompting will cause you to remain under the influence of Christ as you engage in your battle for the day.

In this chapter (and the next three short chapters which follow), I will walk you through how you turn a Spirit-led prompting from your Bible reading into an applied truth in the midst of a difficult circumstance in your daily life. This is what will lead to spiritual victory over the enemy's attacks!

Applying Spirit-led truths to *real time situations* on the same day God gives you the truth is the secret. The proof of a developing personal relation with God is the actual stimulation your inner man receives during your morning walk with Him. Let me repeat this again, because it is the key: Applying Spirit-led truths to *real time situations* on the same day God gives you the truth is the secret.

Your relationship with God is stimulated in your morning walk with Him. It begins with reading, but it must <u>never</u> stop there. Here's why. People often tell me, "Steve, I struggle to read my Bible. I struggle to get alone with God to have devotions. I struggle to have a daily 'God and I' time."

God's Word is like a roadmap, and He will direct your steps with it. Psalm 37:23 says, "The steps of a good man are ordered by the Lord: and he delighteth in his way." The word way means "a course of life." If we allow God to order our steps, then He will be delighted in the course of our lives.

How do you expect God to order your steps? By talking through the television? Or by communicating it over the radio after you hit the snooze button because you're too tired to meet with Him that morning? No, of course not! He will direct you through the Holy Spirit that dwells within your inner man. Your inner man then communicates those steps to your outer man. Your soul's submission to that communication gives direction to your body to follow those "steps of the Lord."

When you accepted Jesus as your personal Savior, His Holy Spirit took up residence within you. John 16:13 says that the Holy Spirit "will guide you into all truth." However He cannot guide you in your course of life if you are not reading the roadmap. Your course of life is the way you choose to live your life moment by moment. Those choices need to be made by following God's roadmap and His intuitive leading on a daily basis.

There are four distinct things that we need to do with God's Word on a daily basis. The first one is to read it! Unfortunately, many people stop right there. Paul said, "Till I come, give attendance (pay attention) to reading, to exhortation, to doctrine." (I Tim. 4:13) Paul's direction for Timothy's ministry was for him to give attendance to reading.

When a schoolteacher takes attendance, she is accounting for each student's daily appointment to his class. Similarly, you should show up for your daily appointment in the Word. The good news is that you are not the only person attending this session. The Holy Spirit will also be there, ready to give you direction.

There is a big misconception concerning reading the Bible. Many people believe that simply reading the Bible will develop a growing relation with God that will lead to prosperity. However, nowhere in Scripture do we see God promise to prosper Bible reading Christians. Nowhere! You can look but you will not find it.

It's not in Joshua 1:8. It's not in Psalm 1:3. God's promise of prosperity is not given to Bible *reading* Christians but to those who *meditate* on the Scriptures! Simply put, we should approach reading the Bible as a means to mediation. Though reading without daily meditation is not a waste of time, such reading is not a means to develop a closer relationship with God.

It is not realistic to expect to just start reading and immediately find yourself in a position where you might maintain a spirit of mediation on what you have just read. There is a method that should be followed in order to develop that spirit of meditation. We have put together what many people have told us is one of the best tools they have ever seen to maximize these steps to walking with God. It's called the Reformers Unanimous *It's Personal* Daily Journal. I

NOWHERE IN SCRIPTURE DO WE SEE GOD PROMISE TO PROSPER BIBLE READING CHRISTIANS.

strongly recommend that you get a copy of this journal and follow the instructional CD that comes with it. This tool has helped tens of thousands of Christians to develop a dynamic, personal, every day walk with God. (The following three chapters lay out this "method toward meditation.")

First, you must be committed to reading your Bible, not *on* purpose but *with* purpose. It is not merely the reading that will help you grow, but rather the application of your reading. We've already discussed the difference between the acquisition of information and the development of a personal relation. The devil uses our desire for information to hinder our walk with God.

The Bible is information about God. However it is also quick—meaning alive! The Bible is powerful. Those descriptions, alive and powerful, also apply to the Spirit who lives within your inner man. Thus the Bible could do for you some of the same things that the Holy Spirit can do for you.

It can communicate the direction of God to your soul. However that will only happen through the portal of your inner man. So reading the Bible does not, I repeat does not, develop your personal relation with God! It is powerful information that contains life. Reading the Bible fulfills God's purpose for you to acquire information about Him. What we do with that information determines what God will be able to do through us. This daily acquisition of information about God will be the fuel that our personal relation with God will burn throughout the remainder of the day!

For this fuel to be of use, we must make the investment to acquire it. That investment is the time we spend reading the Bible. Keep in mind that the Bible is a love letter from your Savior. It's important that we maximize the value of the information that the Spirit is trying to give us in our time with God.

As you read, look for principles, truths, stories and series of events that the Lord may use to speak to you. When God reveals something to you, there is your bonanza! It may be something you have seen before but that catches your attention once again. Or it could be something you have never seen before.

Either way, who do you think it is that is revealing this truth to you? Do you think it is the devil? No? Well then, by process of elimination, who, pray tell, do you think it is? Of course it's the Spirit of God! The Holy Spirit is *guiding you into a truth* that He most certainly knows you need in your life *that day!* That is when you should *stop* reading, at least for a few moments.

Imagine a prospector out seeking for gold. He lays out a map and determines that each day he will search one section. If he found gold in section three, would he leave it behind and move on to section four because that was next on the list? Of course not! He would stay right where he found the gold and try to dig deeper to find all that he could right there.

Now if you are trying to finish a "Bible Reading in a Year" program, stopping when you find a truth will slow you down. But trust me, it's worth it! You do not need a large quantity of reading, but rather good quality in your reading. When the Lord does show you something, it gives you an opportunity to stop and take the second important step in developing your personal relation with God through the use of His Word. That second step—studying, is explained in our next chapter.

chapter two

STUDYING YOUR BIBLE —RELATIONAL

WHEN YOU FIND THAT GOLD NUGGET, YOUR PERSONAL BONANZA, TAKE TIME TO STUDY IT OUT AND DETERMINE HOW GOD MAY BE ORDERING YOUR STEPS. Take that little nugget and begin by dissecting it and defining it. That's a term that I use to describe what I do with Bible verses or *passage promptings* from God. It's what I mean when I say "studying the Bible."

It usually takes me two or three minutes to study a verse and fully understand its meaning. I want to clearly see what God intends for me to glean from His Word. By dissecting and defining a verse, I take it apart, define the words and put it back together. This helps me better understand the insight, application or conviction that the Lord is presenting.

I'd like to recommend one of my favorite study tools to you. I use the 1828 Webster's Dictionary. The reason I use that particular dictionary is that it is the closest to the meaning of the defined English language used by the 19th Century translators of the King James Bible. This will help you see the meaning of the old English words they chose to represent the meaning of the Greek and Hebrew words in the ancient manuscripts. (As I matter of fact, I like this dictionary so much we have it available for our students to purchase at our website, www. reformu.com.

I've heard it said that most books are written for our information but the Bible was written for our transformation. This transformation is the end result of the development of a personal relation! However, if you simply read the Bible and go no further, it will only be information. God's intention is to inform us so that He might transform us. He wants to transform our minds through the Word of God. He does this as we read, then study, and then move on from there.

Paul wrote to Timothy, "Study to show thyself approved unto God, a workman that needeth not to be ashamed, rightly dividing the word of truth." (II Tim. 2:15) Let's follow the process of dissecting and defining this verse, both to see what it says to us and to give you an example of the process.

> **study**: set your thoughts on a subject
> **to show thyself approved**: accepted
> **a workman**: laborer
> **that needeth not to be ashamed**: not affected by shame
> **rightly dividing**: dissecting and defining
> **the word of truth**: the Bible

Notice that "dividing the word" is considered studying, and a type of study that is approved by God. God considers this an acceptable way of dividing His Word. We need to *dissect and define* the Word of God.

Notice also that God describes this kind of study as hard work. He calls the person engaged in the process a workman, or laborer. God knows this is much harder than simply reading. That is why it is acceptable to Him. Not only does he approve of this work, but it also comes with great rewards.

As a careful student, you will not be affected by the shame that comes from not being aware of certain truths in your life. Simply put, a better understanding of what we read, gained by study, will lead us toward better preparation for that day's *circumstances of life*.

When I am reading my Bible, I am often prompted in the spirit with something from a particular passage. I immediately *stop and pause* to consider the meaning of the passage. If my intuitive leading does not readily discern the meaning from the words, I will dissect and define it using my 1828 Webster's Dictionary.

I then put those definitions together and rewrite the verse or paraphrase it in my RU *It's Personal* Journal. Then I continue in my Bible reading for the day. I follow that process with every verse in which the Holy Spirit prompts me. I then take all the dissected and defined passages that I was prompted on and begin to work on the third step in the process (which we'll look at in the next chapter).

As we've seen, reading the Bible is strictly informational. It does not develop a personal relation with God anymore than reading a biography of the great evangelist D. L. Moody develops a relationship with him. It simply gives you information about his life. However when you study (which Webster's defines as "setting your thought upon a subject"), you take a piece of information and begin a *short process* of dwelling on it.

As we discussed in the introduction to this section, you dwell in your heart. The purpose of this section is to give you the tools to determine the position of your heart, and to lead Christ to dwell within it. Studying the Bible is a precursor to getting Christ to dwell in your heart. Though it is just for the time you are studying, He has at least dwelt there during that time.

Your time of study places Christ in your heart, but it won't keep Him there. The concluding two steps for utilizing the Bible contain the means for keeping Him there. To review, when you

READING IS INFORMATIONAL—IT INCREASES YOUR INFORMATION ABOUT GOD; STUDY IS RELATIONAL—IT DEVELOPS YOU PERSONAL RELATION WITH HIM.

read the Bible, you are placing the Powerful, Living Truth in your *mind*. When you study the Bible, you are placing the Powerful, Living Truth in your *heart*. Reading is informational—it increases your information about God; study is relational—it develops you personal relation with Him.

The step of dwelling, whether for a moment in study, or for longer periods of mediation (see Chapter Four), will help you develop a personal relation out of the information you have collected. It's not what you know about a person that makes it personal; it's the deeper meaning of what you know that makes it more personal. Study takes you to that deeper meaning of comprehension concerning a truth.

I reiterate that reading your Bible will increase your information about God while studying the Bible will stimulate your personal relation with God. There are still two more steps that you must put that studied information through in order for it to develop an intimacy with God.

Yes, we must first read God's Word. Second, we must study God's Word. Yet those two exercises alone are not enough to help us prosper in developing our personal relation with Him. We must move forward to the third purpose for God's Word—memorization.

chapter three

MEMORIZING YOUR BIBLE
—INFORMATIONAL

IN REVIEW, I WANT TO ASK YOU WHAT THE BIBLE IS REFERRING TO WHEN IT SPEAKS OF THE "HEART"? We've already studied our inner man (where God's mind, will and emotions dwell in the form of the Holy Spirit) and our outer man (where our own mind, will and emotions dwell). The heart is the trigger between these two entities—the spiritual and the carnal.

The heart is what determines which switch will get tripped in a given circumstance. You can best understand the word heart by picturing it equally attached to both our soul and spirit. The heart affects all three parts of our soul—mind, will and emotions.

Most people think of the heart in the context of emotions. It is the symbol for Valentine's Day. We use the term "give our heart away" when we fall in love. But the heart also affects our mind. The Bible says, "For as he thinketh in his heart, so is he." (Pro. 23:7) We think in our hearts, not our heads. If you think right in your heart, you will be right.

Finally, the heart affects our will. The Bible says that Pharaoh's heart was hardened. (Ex. 7:14) That is to say his will was determined not to submit to God's requests and commands through His messenger Moses.

Thus when we are faced with a decision, we can yield to our soul's thinking, or we can yield to the mind of Christ. We can yield to our soul's stubborn will, or we can yield to the will of God. We can respond with a fleshly emotion (frustration, quick-tempered, harshness, meanness, or discord), or we can respond in an emotion of the Spirit (joy, longsuffering, gentleness, goodness, or meekness).

In other words, we can yield to what we think, feel or want in our outer man, or we can yield to what God thinks, feels and wants in our inner man. And every one of those decisions lies within your heart. It is the trigger! Proverbs 4:23 says, "Keep thy heart with all diligence; for out of it are the issues of life."

This verse teaches us the importance of protecting our trigger (the heart) at all times. The phrase "the issues of life" refers to the circumstances we face and the decisions we make. They come from the heart. When you protect your trigger and condition it with Scripture, then it will flip the switch to respond *in the Spirit* to life's trials. However if you leave your heart unprotected and it becomes hardened by sin, then you will flip the switch toward your own thought, desire and emotions rather than God's.

When you memorize the Bible, it is hidden in your trigger—the heart. This keeps you from acting "after the flesh." Psalm 119:11 says, "Thy word have I hid in mine heart, that I might not sin against thee." (However memorization is still not the final step!)

Deuteronomy 11:18 reminds us of the importance of memorizing God's Word. "Therefore shall ye lay up these my words in your heart (your inner trigger of passions) and in your soul (your mind, will and emotions), and bind them for a sign upon your hand, that they may be as frontlets between your eyes." A study of Hebrew customs shows us that the Lord wants us to keep His words ever before us to remain focused on the path on which He has placed us.

Now when God gives you a passage, and you have studied it out (by dissecting, defining, and rewriting it) thus understanding its meaning, purpose in your heart to memorize it! Again, I use the RU "It's Personal" Journal, which has a section to help you with your Bible memorization.

Remember, you do not have to memorize entire verses word for word without error in order to meditate on God's Word (Step Four). Often I'll take the verses that stick out during my reading and studying and paraphrase them in my journal. I will then reduce my paraphrase to bullet points. I will then memorize either those points (by saying them three to five times) or if God leads, I will memorize part or all of the verse itself.

I then take my "daily meds"—the daily meditation cards in the back of my It's Personal Journal, and I write the truths God is prompting me to learn. I then carry those bullet points and partial verses with me wherever I go ("bind them for a sign upon thy hand"), often paper clipped inside my day planner. I refer to them throughout the day ("that they may be as frontlets between thine eyes"). I keep them ready and available, and refer to them often that I may have them in my trigger when adversity strikes and decisions must be made ("that I might not sin against thee").

However, do not miss this next point. It is integral to understanding how to hide Christ in your heart. I **do not** believe that committing small (or large) parts of the Bible to memory is the key to overcoming sinful temptation. Before you respond, please read on and allow me to explain. Many pastors try to get their congregations to memorize a lot of Scripture in hopes of better arming themselves for spiritual battle.

Memorization is a necessary exercise to engage the Sword of the Spirit. However most church people already have committed large portions of the Bible to memory. Why does it seldom help them? Is it because they haven't memorized enough verses? No, it is because memorization is not the end to your Bible time any more than reading is an end. It is the third step of four; a means to God's end.

Perhaps the best way to understand why we need to memorize is by explaining what memorization *does not* do for you. We've already mentioned Psalm 119:11, "Thy word have I hid in mine heart, that I might not sin against thee." Many people completely misunderstand this verse. They think if you memorize enough verses (with no more than two mistakes per verse!) that it will keep you from sin. That is a total misrepresentation of Scripture. You don't memorize in your heart—you memorize in your head! Your brain holds the information you collect in your memory. When we

I DO NOT BELIEVE THAT COMMITTING SMALL (OR LARGE) PARTS OF THE BIBLE TO MEMORY IS THE KEY TO OVERCOMING SINFUL TEMPTATION.

memorize large amounts of Scripture, we increase our—you guessed it, information! However as we've already seen, information does not develop your personal relation.

You see, I have a lot of things about God memorized, but I seldom use them during difficult circumstances in life. If I am *out* from underneath the Spirit's leading, it will not be memorized Scripture that will help me overcome temptation; it will be self-discipline. People praise self-discipline, but it is not a God-pleasing alternative to Spirit discipline.

So what does God mean when He tells us to hide His word in our hearts that we might not sin? The Bible tells us to compare Scripture with Scripture. Psalm 19:14 says, "Let the words of my mouth, and the meditation of my heart be acceptable in thy sight, O Lord, my strength, and my redeemer."

We memorize in our heads, but *we meditate in our hearts*. In other words, memorization is done in the mind, but meditation is done in the trigger—the heart. We find that this is the most important crucible: to hide God's Word in your heart is done in the meditator, not the memorizer! Acquiring information only helps if you are dwelling on it. Dwelling on information about God will develop a personal relation with God.

Now you can see how working in my journal (reading, studying, memorizing and meditating) is preparing me for battle every day. God is giving me the truths I will need to be prepared for my spiritual battles that day (see Eph. 6:14). Bible memorization places this weapon—the Sword (offensive weapon) of the Spirit in my mind, just as a sword is placed in a sheath.

With the truth sheathed in my mind, I am prepared to meditate on it throughout the day in my heart. My heart needs to be under the influence and control of my spirit, not my soul. When my soul controls my heart, it is desperately wicked (Jer. 17:9). When my spirit controls my heart, it is "fixed, trusting in the Lord" (Ps. 112:7).

If I simply memorize Scripture without dwelling on the Word, I have not hidden it in my heart. There may be a lot of good things stored within my memory, however only what I use is, well, useful. When a soldier went to battle in Bible days, he didn't keep his sword in the sheath—it's not much use there! So memorization without use has no value other than acquired information. However if I use what I have learned—meditation before application—*then* "I might not sin against [God]."

In conclusion, the truths that are tucked away in my meditator (heart) from the promptings during my reading become proof of my personal relation throughout the day. Moment by moment, as difficult circumstances arrive, my bullet points and verses that I'm meditating on throughout the day result in Spirit-led actions and reactions. This is an incredible tool for building confidence in your growing relation with God.

Every time you see Him provide a prompting truth in the morning that sustains your walk with Him during the day, your faith in and fear of the Lord will grow. You will find yourself more willing to yield to the Spirit and you will enjoy a Spirit-filled life. None of this will happen if you do not take your daily meds (meditations)!

Such preparation for the day is what leads to prosperity in the Christian life. We must read so that we can study; we must study so that we can memorize; and we must memorize so that we can engage in the final and most important purpose of the Bible—meditation!

chapter four

MEDITATING ON YOUR BIBLE—RELATIONAL

SO WE HAVE LEARNED THAT READING AND MEMORIZATION WILL HELP US ACQUIRE INFORMATION, BUT STUDYING AND MEDITATION WILL HELP DEVELOP OUR PERSONAL RELATION. I have often heard people talk about the Bible and our need to read and memorize, read and memorize. However, I think you can see why studying and meditation are more important than reading and memorization.

Now, you must conclude however, that one comes after the other step by step so that we must follow all four—read so that you can study, study so that you can memorize, memorize so that you can meditate, and meditate so that everything you do will prosper. (Josh. 1:8, Ps. 1:3) What a formula for success!!!

Telling people to read their Bible has often been a cliché used by many to counsel people. The farther they are from God the more we say "well, you just need to read your Bible more." I know people that read their Bible ten hours a day and are still addicted to crack. What do you say to them? We even teach our children in songs that if they read the Bible...that *they will grow, grow, grow.* However, I know people that read their Bible every day and grow, grow, grow—marijuana! What are you going to tell them?

The same is true for the cliché to memorize the Bible. This was all I heard while I was growing up. If I would memorize passages like a good Christian boy, than I would have God's power to resist sin. But it seldom seemed to work. We tell people to memorize their Bible to fight off the devil, yet I know of people in prison that have large parts of the Bible memorized, but yet they fornicate regularly with fellow inmates. Why? Because reading and memorizing will only increase your information—and that doesn't change behavior; only studying and meditating will increase your personal relation and change your conduct.

We have long misrepresented the purpose of memorization. It is not so that a young person might not sin. It is so that young and old alike might meditate on what God has led them to put into their head. Your mind is like the hard drive on a computer. You store all the data of your life on the hard drive of your mind. Everything you put in, both good and bad, is stored on that hard drive.

However, your heart is like a desktop. It represents what is currently open on your hard drive. The devil intends to bring the outside pressure (called oppression) of the things of this world into your life to cause your heart to pull down negative, wrong or improper or even desperately wicked things from your mind's hard drive and open them on your hearts desktop. That's the purpose of outside pressure— to engage your heart to dwell on negative things that will cause you to yield your soul's control to the external pressure.

This will give Satan all the control he needs to hinder your worship and slow your spirit's intuitive leadings. This renders two thirds of your sprit grieved (and grieves the Holy Spirit as well). With only your conscience available for clear communication with God, the devil will sooth you into an apathetic feeling for the things of God. This will render your conscience back to the still small voice of a undeveloped baby Christian like the church of Corinth.

The devil will not at first lead you into deep sin, for surely you would repent and reject that quickly. Rather he will keep you wallowing around in shallow sin. What a defeated and frustrating way to live the Christian life! No wonder many cannot smile as they sing "Victory in Jesus."

I believe the best way to get out from underneath the age old cliché of teaching—read and memorize, read and memorize—is to stop telling people that God will change their life if they will read and memorize. This is especially since most of them have tried all that and He hasn't changed their lives. Rather, let's teach them the truth that God will change their lives if they meditate on His Word. That will get their attention, because they know they haven't been doing that. And they'll try it!

The first time I ever flew in an airplane was on my honeymoon to Cozumel, Mexico, with my wife Lori. My face was pressed against the airplane window throughout the flight as I watched the beautiful landscape below. At one point, we came over what looked to be a stream or river of water. As my eyes traced that stream, I noticed that all the trees on its banks were much larger, greener, and taller than those growing further away.

I immediately thought of Psalm 1:2-3.

"But his delight (or, enjoyment) is in the law of the LORD; and <u>in his law doth he meditate</u> (or, think upon) day and night. And he shall be like a tree planted by the rivers of water, that bringeth forth his fruit in his season; his leaf also shall not wither; and <u>whatsoever he doeth shall prosper.</u>"

A man who meditates on the Bible will be like those trees. His "branches" will extend farther and higher; his growth will be much faster and deeper than those outside the reach of the life-giving water of the river. Fruit-bearing and beautiful, any righteous thing such a man (or woman) does will thrive.

A man who meditates on God's Word delights in God's Word, meaning that he enjoys his meditation. You will too, once you begin seeing the result of your own meditation, that is prosperity in your course of life. The sad truth is, many of us find reading the Word of God something of a chore or minimum requirement for pleasing God. That is not how it should be! It ought to be a delight!

God wants to guide and direct us through His Word so that we might make wise decisions leading to prosperity in specific areas of our lives. He wants to order our steps. He wants us to be grounded, fruitful, and prosperous. But that requires us to delight in God's Law—and that manifests itself through meditation on His Law. You should begin mediatating every morning and continue right through the day and into the night. God will indeed prosper a Christian who is meditating on the Bible!

Enjoyment is simply a matter of appetite. To enjoy something, an appetite for it needs to be created and fed. When I was younger, I hated stuffing. My mother could not get me to eat it, and after many attempts, she finally stopped trying to make me. However, after I got married, Lori consistently tried to get me to eat her mother's stuffing.

She made it regularly and was quite persuasive in her attempts to get me to try it—and like it. Not wanting to upset my new bride, I decided to try her mother's stuffing. It was the first time I could remember actually even tasting stuffing. After all those years, I came to realize that I had never really tried to like it. I simply rejected it and, as a result, I had no appetite for it.

Well, as you've probably already guessed, I really liked it. (Sorry, Mom! Nothing personal.) As a result, Lori increased the frequency at which she served stuffing, and I developed an appetite for it that often leads me to be, well…quite stuffed!

Reading the Bible is the same way. We don't have a strong appetite for it, but that's because we have never really tasted the finished product made according to God's recipe—meditation used for *real time* application. Oh, we may read it, skimming through it like we are picking at food with a fork. But we fail to really take the time to try it and like it. As a result, nothing changes.

When we take the time to read, study, memorize, and meditate on God's Word, we will see Him at work in our lives. We will be able to see that God is directing our steps as we exercise the four-fold purpose of His Word. This will excite us! We will become delighted in the way in which He is leading us. It will lead to prosperity and our "God and I" time will, as a result, become intensely personal and intimate—and something we look forward to rather than dread. This exercise in God's Word is sure to increase our appetite for God's Word and we *will* be delighted in it.

Read so you may study what God shows you. Study so you may understand its meaning. Memorize so you can remember what God has shown you. Meditate so you will be prepared to apply the two-edged Sword in the time of adversity. Doing these four things is the first step of strengthening your inner man. A strengthened inner man will be the conduit of an intimate personal walk with God.

Let's stop telling people that their life will prosper if they read their Bibles. Many people are or have read the Bible, and yet they have failed and failed. Let's teach people instead that if they meditate on their Bibles then EVERYTHING they do will prosper and succeed. It's a promise from Scripture that our family, friends and fellow Christians really need.

> "This book of the law shall not depart out of thy mouth; but thou shalt <u>meditate</u> therein day and night, that thou <u>mayest</u> observe to do according to all that is written therein: <u>for then thou shalt make thy way prosperous</u>, and then thou shalt have good success." -Joshua 1:8

My conclusion after studying this matter is that it is IMPOSSIBLE for the devil to mentally, psychologically, or spiritually enslave a Bible-meditating Christian. However, I have seen quite a few enslaved Bible readers. You've probably seen the same thing in your own life.

In order for you to dwell on Christ, as our verses in Ephesians 3 told us, you must be strengthened in your inner man by His Spirit. How does He do this? He arms us with Scriptures given by Christ and dwelt on in your heart. Then He places you in difficult circumstances so as to force you to use those meditations to increase our faith.

Let's read again these key verses from Ephesians 3:14-19:

"For this cause I...would grant you, according to the riches of his glory, to be <u>strengthened</u> with might <u>by his Spirit in the inner man</u>; That <u>Christ may dwell in your hearts by faith</u>; that ye, being rooted and grounded in love, May be able to comprehend with all saints what is the breadth, and length, and depth, and height; And to know the love of Christ, which passeth knowledge, that ye might be filled with all the fulness of God."

In chapters one through four, we have taught you how to get Christ to dwell in your heart—your meditator. The next four chapters will discuss how to strengthen your faith so that the truths of Christ will remain in your heart. He will only dwell, or remain, in your meditator if you have faith—real faith. But there are many measures of faith. How much faith does it take to get Christ to consistently remain within your meditator? That is our next topic.

chapter five

REAFFIRMING YOUR HELPLESSNESS

"I AM CRUCIFIED WITH CHRIST: NEVERTHELESS I LIVE; YET NOT I, BUT CHRIST LIVETH IN ME: AND THE LIFE WHICH I NOW LIVE IN THE FLESH I LIVE BY THE FAITH OF THE SON OF GOD, WHO LOVED ME, AND GAVE HIMSELF FOR ME. I do not frustrate the grace of God: for if righteousness come by the law, then Christ is dead in vain."-Galatians 2:20-21

Knowing God is the absolutely essential ingredient of the abundant Christian life. In this chapter, we will discover the key to understanding and applying this absolute truth to your personal walk with God. Galatians 2:20 is not only the key verse to this chapter, but it is the key verse to the next four chapters, as well. In fact, it is not an exaggeration to say that Galatians 2:20 is the key to your complete understanding, application, and experiencing the abundant Christian life.

You see, we are dead; nevertheless we live. This appears to be a contradiction, but understanding this truth will let us live freely in this bound world. Here is how it should be done. As a result of our new birth, or what the Bible calls being "born again," we have a new existence that is being offered for our experience and enjoyment.

Our key verses in Galatians teach us several things about our new life in Christ. They first teach us that we are helpless. As a matter of fact, we have been put to death ("I am crucified with Christ..."). Sometimes we may forget that we are dead. Dead people cannot help themselves. There will be times when we will have to **reaffirm our helplessness**. That will be the main thrust of this chapter.

While teaching us to reaffirm our helplessness, these verses also lead us to **realize our new identity in Christ** ("nevertheless I live;

yet not I, but Christ liveth in me…"). We will discuss this in the next chapter. Our former helplessness is replaced with Christ whose power is limitless. To elevate our potential from helpless to limitless, we must **recognize the power of faith** ("the life which I now live in the flesh I live by the faith of the Son of God."). We will examine the power of faith in Chapter Seven, and in Chapter Eight, we'll see how you can **register a full measure of faith**.

Our final act of submission requires a willingness to **relinquish self-ownership** of our lives to the Christ who wants to live His life through us ("[He] who loved me, and gave himself for me"). We'll discuss this concept in chapter nine. Having been crucified yet living, we can by faith submit to the inner man's leading.

The goal of our Christian life is to grow in our faith of God's finished work, so that His work will not remain finished! What I mean by that is that God wants to continue His Work in your life until His return. (Phil. 1:6) In order to do this, He must live His life through our submitted soul in the power of our strengthened inner man. The only thing that develops and strengthens this inner man, as we saw in our Ephesians 3, is faith.

If you recall, we learned in Section Two Chapter Nine that faith is a measurement. Just like your weight is a measurement of how much you weigh and your height is a measurement of how tall you are, your faith is a measurement as well. Your faith is a measurement of the level of confidence you have in what Christ did for you (leading to the benefits of justification) and what He wants to do through you (leading to the benefits of sanctification).

So, based on our behavior, others will be able to somewhat effectively measure our faith. However, God looks on the heart. He investigates your meditator. He can determine if we are *transforming* while in the midst of a trial of our faith or if we are *performing* in the midst of our trial. The result of this investigation will show the Lord a faith that is growing or a faith that is doubting.

If your faith is growing, you can be sure that your new levels will bring new devils. Yet while you experience more trials, you can be sure that your growing faith in your personal relationship with Christ will get your through the storm. It becomes reciprocal, like compounding interest. The more trials you experience and weather successfully, the more your faith grows. The more your faith grows, the more you can and will do for God. The more you do for God, the more the devil will try to gain control of your soul through outside pressure (oppression).

However, if you have weak faith, you are not pleasing God. It's impossible to please Him apart from faith. (Heb. 11:6) If your faith is weak, God is going to put you in positions that will force you to depend wholly on Him. However, if you have weak faith, you will often fail these tests and find yourself frustrated.

God's desire is that your frustration will cause you to investigate your own heart and see your weak faith. As you come to recognize that your weak faith is a by-product of a weak relationship, then you will begin to restore or develop that weakened relationship with Him. As you obey conscience-led conviction, your worship will evolve into clear communication from God's Word. As you meditate on the Word, your intuition will bring it to remembrance during times of

IF YOUR FAITH IS WEAK, GOD IS GOING TO PUT YOU IN POSITIONS THAT WILL FORCE YOU TO DEPEND WHOLLY ON HIM.

urgent need. You will apply that truth and overcome in the power of the Holy Spirit during a particular trial.

The process of growth then begins. If you are humble and realize that God has done that great work for you and through you, than your faith will grow. He will become more real to you, and your faith-building sessions will begin to become reciprocal, returning many benefits regularly. Yet, if you become proud at the conclusion of a successful endurance of a trial, you will see your conscience offended, your worship will weaken and your intuition be minimalized.

To understand the steps to the abundant Christian life, you must realize the importance of faith. Paul said the life he now lived he lived by the faith of the Son of God. Faith—that's the same thing that saved me! So we see that faith must have different measurements. There is a level of faith that saves and a level of faith that changes and maybe other levels in between.

I want to discuss this by first taking some time to explain this key verse that explains, in just a few short sentences the abundant Christian life. In verse 21, Paul shows us that we are capable of slowing God's work in us; we can be guilty of putting on the brakes. We can throw a monkey wrench in the works and mess up the Lord's design, effectively quenching the Holy Spirit in our lives.

We frustrate the grace of God by trying to obtain any level of righteousness by observing the Old Testament law (works). Grace is when God is doing all the work; the law is when man is doing the work. "Frustrate" means to violate or neutralize, rendering to a state of indifference. Paul is telling us that when we try to do the work of God in the power of our own flesh, we violate God's grace. We neutralize it.

God's grace in your life is dependent on you yielding your dead works to His living work within you. When you try to do good in the flesh, you set aside Christ's death and His continuing work. His sacrifice is in vain and His grace is frustrated. Your new life in Christ will suffer. Remember, God's power in your life is only limited by your fleshly efforts.

Do you find yourself in this position? You are not alone. The Apostle Paul found himself in this same position often. He had to *reaffirm his helplessness* regularly by dying not once, but on a daily basis (I Cor. 15:31). He had to *realize his identity* in Christ over and over again, as he considered himself the chief of sinners (I Tim. 1:15). He struggled to *recognize the power of faith*, so God gave him a weakness that hampered him so much that he, "besought the Lord...that it might depart from [him]." (II Cor. 12:8).

But the Lord wanted him to see God's power and thus increase his faith. Paul's eventual conclusion was that, "when I am weak, then am I strong." (II Cor. 12:10) He would once again *relinquish self-ownership* to God in order "that the power of Christ might rest upon [him]." (II Cor. 12:9)

Some say the Apostle Paul was the best Christian that ever lived, yet even he needed to be reminded of the power of his faith regularly. Do not be discouraged if you also need to be reminded once in a while. God understands that we are accustomed to doing our own work our own way. That began in the Garden of Eden and will continue until He returns.

To avoid frustrating or neutralizing the grace of God, than we must begin by reaffirming our helplessness. Paul says in our key verse for these next four chapters, "I am crucified with Christ." But for dead people, we sure cause ourselves a lot of problems, don't we?

We would do well if we would remember our position in Christ. We died with Him. Romans 6:6-7 says, "Knowing this, that our old man is crucified with him, that the body of sin might be destroyed, that henceforth we should not serve sin. For he that is dead is freed from sin." The "body of sin" is not a person; it is a ruling authority. We are born as servants to sin. When a person dies, his ability to serve is eliminated.

God's purpose for our spiritual death (which precedes our spiritual re-birth) is to take away our ruler (sin) and its governing power. This master within us must be subdued, weakened, and placed under the restraints of our new ruler, Christ. The body of sin, like the body of Christ, has many members. Members simply means "body parts!" Those body parts are naturally under the rule of sin. God's desire is for us to die like and with Christ, so that sin's members and its deeds will be mortified, or put to death.

Our problem is not so much our continuing struggle with sin that slows our progress in the Christian walk. That's where most people focus, but they're looking in the wrong direction. The real problem is that we fail to serve our new governing Authority. We tend to believe that we can do good without following our new Ruler.

When we do this, we not only frustrate God's grace (God's great plan for us), but we also frustrate ourselves. We fail to achieve the progress in our Christian lives that we had hoped to achieve by our righteous living, and we become discouraged with ourselves. We forget that, being dead, we are helpless without this new and pure, living Authority ruling our lives.

In Romans 7:24, Paul cried out in frustration, "O wretched man that I am! who shall deliver me from the body of this death?" Without God, we are nothing. Yet, we often foolishly attempt to accomplish our good works or make great feats of righteous living in our own strength. Before God can do anything with us, we must first come to the conclusion that without God's power on us, we are helpless.

Without submission to His rule over our lives, we are helpless in overcoming the strongholds that sin (our former ruler) attempts to bring back into our lives. The power to gain such victories comes **only** through Christ living in us. His rule over us gives us the strength we need to resist the lure and allure of our former ruler. A verse so often quoted, Philippians 4:13, says, "I can do all things through Christ which strengtheneth me." Oh, how often we forget how helpless we are without the strength of Christ!

When I was running from the Lord and my addictions were crippling my life, I would cry out to God, "Why did You let this happen to me? Why won't You protect me from the devil? Can't You take away this temptation?" But, I had put myself in that position–not God. Galatians 6:7-8 says, "Be not deceived (or, misled); God is not mocked (or, imitated): for whatsoever a man soweth (or, scatters), that shall he also reap. For he that soweth to his flesh shall of the flesh reap corruption; but he that soweth to the Spirit shall of the Spirit reap life everlasting." Let's dissect this verse and define the words so that we can have a greater understanding of what God is trying to teach us.

Be not deceived (or, misled); God is not mocked (or, imitated). How do we try to imitate God? We imitate God when we live as if we control the consequences for our wrongdoings. I made this mistake many times in my early flight to find freedom. I would go out for the evening, planning to enjoy myself. Yet I knew that if I allowed myself to walk out the door, I was going to do something before the night was over that was against the law and a sin against God.

I knew that I would struggle with drugs and alcohol. However, I foolishly believed that if I controlled the atmosphere in which I indulged in these sinful things, somehow I could control the consequences of it. If I could keep myself from drinking too much, then I would not get a DUI. I could participate in drugs but hide it well enough so the cops would not find out.

I was convinced that I could control the consequences of my choices. I was mocking God. I was imitating God by acting as if I had the power to control each and every circumstance. But, who truly is in control of everything? God is, of course. I lived as if I had no ruling Authority within me. I forgot I was helpless.

...for whatsoever a man soweth **(or, scatters),** *that shall he also reap* **(or, receive in return).** Farming is the best example of the Law of Sowing and Reaping. When a farmer goes to his field to plant his crop, he *sows* his seed. Figuratively speaking, that is what we do as we live out our lives. We leave distinctive paths behind us. Those paths are what we have sown.

The seed will then ripen until harvest. It always does; it never fails. We will reap the fruit of whatever seed we sow. If a farmer plants corn, he will not reap green beans. So, the produce of whatever a man leaves scattered behind him is exactly what that man will eventually receive. Galatians 6:8 goes on to say, "For he that soweth to his flesh (or, desires) shall of the flesh reap corruption (or, ruin); but he that soweth to the Spirit shall of the Spirit reap life everlasting."

The man that lives for his own desires will reap ruin, but the man that lives under the control of the Holy Spirit (his new Ruler) will reap an abundant life. You are responsible for where you are today. You are reaping what you have previously sown. Do not be misled. God is not going to be imitated.

Everyone of us will either choose to follow our former ruler and reap ruin, or we will choose to follow the new Ruler within us and reap life. For whatever we leave behind in our lives, we will receive back the results of those same deeds. We are helpless. We cannot live righteously without yielding to our new Ruler, and we will not live sinfully without first submitting to our former ruler.

Our willingness to submit to the leading of our former ruler is what put us in this position of helplessness–not God; He is our helper. "Helper" is one of the definitions of the Comforter (see John 14:16-18). He will help us reap life if we will sow submission to Him.

Let's take a look at the descending path of sowing to the flesh. First, we were deceived. You may ask, "How could I allow the devil to deceive me?" It's very simple. You see, Satan sows and reaps, too. When the devil plants a deceitful thought in your heart, you have the option to either accept it or reject it. The choice is yours alone whether to be deceived or not.

Proverbs 3:5 says, "Trust in the LORD with all **thine heart**; and lean not unto thine own understanding." When you give consideration to a deceitful thought and begin reasoning within yourself to justify it, you are handing the devil a building permit to start immediate construction of a stronghold in your mind. This will always lead to corruption in your heart. (Remember, your heart is the seat of belief.)

The Bible indicates that a stronghold in the mind exists when we choose to believe something which contradicts the Word of God (see 2 Corinthians 10:3-5). Hebrews 3:12 says, "Take heed, brethren, lest there be in any of you an evil heart of unbelief, in departing from the living God." It is very easy to be deceived when you stop believing the Truth. That is why we are so helpless without God.

After we are deceived, we then sow our seed. Second Corinthians 9:6 says, "He which soweth sparingly shall reap also sparingly; and he which soweth bountifully shall reap also bountifully." If we have bountifully scattered seeds of destruction behind us, we will reap that same destruction at some point in our lives. (And by the way, you always reap *more* than you sow!)

I have made many bad decisions. In every case, those decisions were the result of errors in my thinking. I was thinking with my deceived mind and it led to me yielding to the wrong authority. The key to sowing the right seed is yielding to the inner man rather than the outer man. By God's grace, I finally realized I needed to change my decision-making process. Seeing my need for guidance and direction, I began looking to God's Word to lead me in my decisions. Heeding the Bible helps us avoid Satanic deception.

As we discussed in our last chapter, Hebrews 4:12 says, "For the word of God is quick, and powerful, and sharper than any twoedged sword, piercing even to the dividing asunder of soul and spirit, and of the joints and marrow, and is a discerner of the thoughts and intents of the heart." The key to the work of the Word in your life is the piercing and dividing of the soul (outer man) from the spirit (inner man).

God's Word intends to separate your soul (mind, will, and emotions) and your spirit (God in you). Sometimes when God is giving us a leading, we begin to think about His direction. We begin to rationalize His will.

THE KEY TO SOWING THE RIGHT SEED IS YIELDING TO THE INNER MAN RATHER THAN THE OUTER MAN.

Our emotions can begin to get involved and our stubborn will reacts to His leading. Before we know it, our souls have cancelled out the Spirit's leading. We have taken God's thoughts or God's will or God's emotions and we have contaminated them with our selfish thoughts, desires, or feelings.

When we are making decisions apart from His Word, we may be deceived by our own judgment. But if we run to God's Word for our answers, He will separate our deceived hearts from His clear direction. The Bible will point out areas in our lives that need to be changed. God's Word is, "a discerner of the thoughts and intents of the heart." Your heart may not always tell you the truth, but the Word will.

To protect yourself from being deceived, which leads to sowing the wrong seed, check your emotions, your thoughts, and your desires with the Bible. That's where your answers will be found. Remember 2 Timothy 3:16? "All scripture is given by inspiration of God, and is profitable for doctrine, for reproof, for correction, for instruction in righteousness:" The Bible's purpose is to show us what is right (doctrine), what is not right (reproof), how to get right (correction), and how to stay right (instruction in righteousness).

So, the first step to getting Christ to dwell within our hearts by faith is to reaffirm our helplessness. Before God can do anything with our lives, we must reaffirm that without the help of God and His Word, we are helpless. But there is hope! You have the means to protect yourself from deception by seeking God's guidance through the Bible.

chapter six

REALIZE YOUR NEW IDENTITY IN CHRIST

TO STRENGTHEN OUR FAITH, IT'S NOT ENOUGH TO SIMPLY RECOGNIZE WE ARE HELPLESS, FOR THAT WOULD SIMPLY SADDEN US TO RECON OURSELVES OF NO EXISTENCE. We must also **realize our new identity in Christ.** Paul goes on in Galatians 2:20 to encourage us that, even though we have been crucified with Christ and are helpless, "nevertheless I live; yet not I, but Christ liveth in me."

When we were crucified with Christ, our subordinate members were no longer under obligation to submit to the ruling authority of sin. Rather, we were re-created in the image of Christ. Our members are now instructed by the Word of Truth and the Spirit of Truth to submit to our new ruling Authority. This is how God wants us to live. The Spirit of God that has quickened (made alive) your spirit will now guide you and direct you into all truth (Ps. 32:8).

Submission to this inner Leader is referred to in our key verses as Christ living in us. That is the manifestation of our new creation in Christ. We are no longer forced into submission to the body of sin. Instead, we are given the opportunity to yield in submission to the indwelling Holy Spirit. We do not have to work our way to righteousness in our own power. God is leading us into the paths of righteousness, and He is doing it for His name's sake! (Ps. 23:3)

In 2 Corinthians 5:17 Paul records this truth concerning the regime change within us: "Therefore if any man be in Christ, he is a new creature: old things are passed away; behold, all things are become new." I have heard people argue that this verse is not referring to the "old man" passing away and a "new man" coming alive, but rather it is referring to the old covenant (the law) passing away and the new covenant (grace) replacing it. I would tend to agree that, in context, this is referring to the end of the law and the replacement of God's new covenant of grace.

However, the truth of this passage is just as real regardless of which view is being discussed here. Paul is telling us that since we are in Christ, we are literally new creatures. The old covenant of man doing the work is passed away and has been replaced with the new covenant where God does the work. Amen!

I am so sick of this "try hard to do better" mentality that is permeating our churches and Christian schools. It is why Christianity is so attacked by the seldom churched with charges of legalism. When it comes to justification, we all agree that Christ *did* the work, but when it comes to sanctification, we somehow believe that we must paddle our own canoe.

We often believe the ability to live righteously is found in our effort and will power. This is not true. This view is called legalistic sanctification. Christ's substitionary death paid our penalty for sin and emancipated us from the power of sin. Christ's death paid our penalty; Christ's resurrection freed us from sin's power. A paid penalty is justification; emancipation is sanctification.

When we fail to understand our new identity in Christ, we lose focus on how to walk in victory. We are not so much required to do well as we are requested to yield to His leading. John 15:7 says, "If ye abide in me...ye shall ask what ye will, and it shall be done unto you." In effect Jesus was saying, "If you cooperate with Me, things will happen for your benefit."

He is willing to lead a cooperative subordinate. He will not force you to follow Him. If you know His voice is calling, you should follow. It is a wonderful privilege to be a Christian! When we understand God's management system, we will better understand who we are and how He intends to use us. In Section One, we discussed this understanding process as coming to realize our need to transform our minds. *Transform* means "to metamorphose; to change the character, nature, condition, etc., of something or someone."

"Don't make me angry. You wouldn't like me when I'm angry."
Remember the illustration we shared earlier? In the early 1980s I enjoyed watching a television show called *The Incredible Hulk*. It was the comic book story of David Bruce Banner... "Physician...

Scientist… searching for a way to tap into the hidden strength that all humans have, when an accidental overdose of gamma-radiation altered his body chemistry. And now, when David Banner becomes angry or outraged, a startling metamorphosis occurs…" They would then close the show's introduction with a view of David Banner becoming angry after injuring himself while changing a flat tire during a storm. Then, turning into a green, muscle-bound monster, he would beat up his car.

Though a silly story, there is a profound truth in this illustration. You see, when God transforms our minds, we begin to understand who we really are in Christ. Our identity in Christ is personally experienced. This position (in which we do not rule, but rather submit to Him) allows us to experience a startling

WHEN IT COMES TO JUSTIFICATION, WE ALL AGREE THAT CHRIST DID THE WORK, BUT WHEN IT COMES TO SANCTIFICATION, WE SOMEHOW BELIEVE THAT WE MUST PADDLE OUR OWN CANOE.

metamorphosis during times of adversity when, in the past, we may have become frustrated or angry.

Realizing our new identity, we may submit to a power greater than ours, one through which we will respond correctly to difficult circumstances. This metamorphosis is Christ in us, *the hope of glory* (Colossians 1:27). *Glory* means "to bring the right opinion of." It literally means to make someone look good. Christ living in us is our only hope of ever looking good when adversity strikes.

God's purpose for us looking good is that we might make Him look good in the process. In other words, we glorify God (make Him look good) when others see this startling metamorphosis occur in our lives. Society tells us that **behavior determines belief.** If you behave a certain way, you are providing insight into your belief system.

If you are a drinker, then you believe that drinking is acceptable behavior; if you smoke dope, then you believe there is nothing wrong with drug use; if you live immorally, then you do not believe in the importance of moral purity; if you criticize others, then you are showing that you believe there is nothing wrong with giving evil reports. This is the system of the world–behavior determines belief.

God, however, has created a different management system. His system teaches us that **belief should determine behavior**. For example, if a young woman of the night–a harlot, if you will–were to be introduced to a king and fell in love with him, you might think it an odd thing. And if that king subsequently fell in love with this harlot, you might think it even more odd.

But if these two unlikely candidates for love were to marry and move into his royal castle, do you think she would continue her trade of prostitution when darkness falls upon the city streets? No way! She would find her former behavior detestable. Why? Because she is no longer a prostitute. She is a queen! She is the wife of a king. How perverse and profane it would be if she ever went back to living like a harlot! She is going to behave differently because she rightly believes that her nature has changed. No longer is she a "business" woman; she is a lady of the highest order.

It is the same for you and for me. We have been adopted into a new family. We are children of the King of Kings. That makes us royalty in His heavenly kingdom where Jesus is preparing a place for us. He has been working on it for nearly two thousand years. If He can create the splendor of the universe in just six literal days, imagine how marvelous our home in Heaven must be by now. And because I *believe* this, I *behave* differently than I used to. You ought to as well.

Your new identity—who you are in Christ is supposed to determine how you behave. Often after conversion, new believers go from being ruled by the body of sin to trying to live righteously in their own power. The proper way to behave is predicated on understanding who you are in Christ–your new identity. You are His.

He leads, you submit, and a supernatural power to face the circumstances of life is the guaranteed result. That is who you are in Christ. It is as simple as follow the leader. We followed the leader (our father, the devil) before our conversion. Now we must resist the temptation to self-rule. Spirit-rule is the key to the dynamic Christian walk.

chapter seven

RECOGNIZE THE POWER OF FAITH

FIRST WE MUST REGULARLY REAFFIRM THAT WE ARE HELPLESS AS DEAD PEOPLE. Then we must realize that we are alive as conduits of the Lord Jesus Christ. Next we simply need to have a level of confidence in these facts. God *can* and *will* live His crucified life through us, <u>if</u> we will simply recognize that power through faith. Paul goes on to tell us in Galatians 2:20 that, "the life which I now live in the flesh I live by the faith of the Son of God."

Now, of course, understanding that Christ is in us and willing to lead us is not too difficult to accept. However, merely accepting this truth does not produce change. *Belief* is what produces change. Belief in Christ's substitutionary death on the cross is what grants us justification; belief in Christ's substitutionary placement in us is what provides us with sanctification. Faith saves, and faith produces change. We are so certain of the requirement of faith to produce a convert, but we often overlook the need for faith in Christ's leading in order to produce a changed life.

In our key verse, I am reminded that the life that I now live must be lived by faith—not faith in myself or in my church or in my works, but faith in the very same Son of God who saved my soul from Hell. Praise God! His gift of salvation keeps on giving!

What exactly is faith? I have some people define faith as a bold obedience to God's revealed will despite all circumstances. That may be the definition for the level of faith that changes you, but it is not the definition of the faith that saves you. Obedience doesn't produce regeneration, it is faith that produces regeneration. Thus, faith has two definitions, or measurements.

There is the faith that saves you and the faith that changes you. I define faith as, "the personal measurement of my level of confidence in what Christ can and will do in, through, and for us." When you exercise your faith, you are saying, "I am doing this because I believe the result will be exactly what God says it will be." Each time we go through this exercise, it produces a greater measure of faith.

As we saw in Section One, God's will is revealed through our **presentation**, **conformation**, and **transformation**. (Rom. 12:1-2) When His will is revealed, then real faith is measured by our willingness to step out in *bold* obedience and do as God directs, regardless of the circumstances.

It is important to understand this vital truth: God's acceptance of us <u>cannot</u> be acquired by what we have done for Him, nor can it be lost by what we have failed to do. We receive God's acceptance by having faith in His sacrifice for justification and faith in His guidance for sanctification. There are three aspects of faith that we need to understand to properly exercise our faith.

FAITH DEPENDS ON ITS OBJECT.

Many people have faith in faith itself, rather than faith in an object. Your faith should be 100% dependent on the object in which you are placing that faith. If you have faith that a chair will hold your weight, then you have placed your faith in the object–the chair. You believe it will hold you up, so you exercise that belief by sitting in it. Many self-help programs in society will tell you to pick something or someone in which to place your faith.

If you place your faith in something besides God's system of management, then you will have made the same mistake as those in society who are "Having a form of godliness, but denying the power thereof: from such turn away." (II Tim. 3:5) Place your faith in Christ alone, both to save you and to lead you. Faith in God is "the substance of things hoped for, the evidence of things not seen." (Heb. 11:1)

THE DEPTH OF OUR FAITH IS DETERMINED BY THE DEPTH OF OUR KNOWLEDGE OF THE OBJECT IN WHICH WE PLACE OUR FAITH.

Do you need more faith? Then gain more knowledge of your object of faith–God. Romans 10:17 says, "So then faith cometh by hearing, and hearing by the word of God." Your faith and knowledge of God will grow as you are under the teaching and preaching of the Word of God.

I have two friends named John and Michael. John has been my friend for years. I just met Michael a few months ago. I have a lot of knowledge about John, however, I only know a little bit about Michael. If I needed to lend a one dollar bill to either of them, it would not take much effort on my part to exercise this measure of faith . I have little knowledge of Michael, but I would still be willing to lend him something of so little value. However, if I had $100,000 in my pocket and I needed to find someone to entrust it to, I'm going to give it to John. That's because I have more knowledge of him and can exercise my faith *in* him based on my knowledge *of* him.

Similarly, our faith in God is based on how much knowledge we have of Him. If God asks us for a little, then we oblige Him. If God asks for much, then we hold back. Romans 12:1-2 begs us to give our lives to Him as a living sacrifice. We look at our life as being worth $100,000 and are unwilling to yield. God looks at our life as being worthless and the next life as being of great value.

In Luke 9:24 Jesus said, "Whosoever will save his life shall lose it: but whosoever will lose his life for my sake, the same shall save it." Because we do not know God well, we are unwilling to make a sacrifice above our current measure of confidence in Him. Our sacrifice is limited, not by what He can do with us, but by what we fail to believe. We do not recognize the power of faith in our lives.

Hebrews 11:6 says, "But without faith it is impossible to please him: for he that cometh to God must believe that he is, and

WE LOOK AT OUR LIFE AS BEING WORTH $100,000 AND ARE UNWILLING TO YIELD. GOD LOOKS AT OUR LIFE AS BEING WORTHLESS AND THE NEXT LIFE AS BEING OF GREAT VALUE.

that he is a rewarder of them that diligently seek him." Our ability to please God is <u>directly</u> related to our faith in Him. When we come to God, we must come *in faith,* believing in who God is and believing that He will reward our diligence in seeking Him.

When we desire our will over God's will, we are not exercising faith in God. We have all been guilty of searching for God's direction and then, having been shown His direction, doubting our ability to follow it. Maybe God points out areas of our lives that need to change, or He may call us to the mission field or to change careers. God's pleasure in us comes to a halt the moment we choose to follow our own will with disregard to His direction. At that moment, we cease from exercising faith. We often want God's favor on our lives as a prerequisite to increasing our faith in Him. But it doesn't work that way. The step of faith comes first, then the reward.

FAITH IS AN ACTION WORD—NOT PASSIVE.

Faith says, "I am going to *do* right." James 2:17-18 says, "Even so faith, if it hath not works, is dead, being alone. Yea, a man may say, Thou hast faith, and I have works: show me thy faith without thy works, and I will show thee my faith by my works." Our outward actions reveal the inner condition of our faith. "Works" is an old English word for the Modern English word "effort." Our efforts do not save us, neither do they change us, but they are a by-product of our faith. Faith without works (effort) is dead. We need to recognize faith's power and then exercise that measure of faith.

Matthew 14:25-31 gives us the account of Peter walking on the water. The disciples were out to sea in the middle of the night when a strong storm came. In the midst of the storm, Jesus came walking on the water toward them. They thought He was a ghost! But in verse 27 we read, "Jesus spake unto them, saying, Be of good cheer; it is I; be not afraid."

Peter's response was, "Lord, if it be thou, bid me come unto thee on the water. And [Jesus] said, Come. And when Peter was come down out of the ship, he walked on the water, to go to Jesus." (Matt. 14:28&29) Peter's faith was put in action by his immediate obedience to God's call, despite the potential consequences.

The Bible goes on to say in verses 30 and 31, "But when he saw the wind boisterous, he was afraid; and beginning to sink, he cried, saying, Lord, save me. And immediately Jesus stretched forth his hand, and caught him, and said unto him, O thou of little faith, wherefore didst thou doubt?"

When Peter's eyes were focused on Jesus, he was able to walk on top of the water *in faith*. But as soon as he took his eyes off of Jesus and put them on the circumstances around him, he began to sink. When we take our eyes off of Jesus, our faith is going to waver. Friend, our faith is based on nothing less than Jesus' blood (for justification) and righteousness (for sanctification). You have died to the power of sin.

You are now helpless to live righteously without your new identity—Christ in you. Recognize that these truths will change your life *if* you will only believe them.

Determining your level of faith is as simple as determining your weight or your height. It is just another measurement. Faith is a measurement of your confidence in God. This confidence is not only in Him to save you, but to change you as well. Do you believe? All things are possible to them that believe. (Mark 9:23) In our next chapter we will discuss how to measure our confidence in Him, that is to say how to take a measurement of your faith. Having done that, we will explain how you can register a full measure of faith that will please God.

chapter eight

REGISTERING A FULL MEASURE OF FAITH

I WOULD LIKE TO STEP AWAY FROM GALATIANS 2:20 FOR THIS CHAPTER TO TAKE THE TIME TO DIG DEEPER INTO THE TRUTHS TAUGHT IN THE LAST CHAPTER. Our text for Section Three, Ephesians 3, reminds us that to enjoy the fullness of God we *must* be strengthened by His Spirit in the inner man. This happens as we bring Christ into our hearts through meditation and when we continue to dwell in Him through faith.

The faith Paul is taking about in Ephesians 3 is the same measure of faith he is talking about in Galatians 2:20. Yet it is a different measure of faith than he is talking about in Ephesians 2:8&9, which is a faith that saves you. In Galatians 2:20 he is talking about a faith that changes you. They are different measures.

In this chapter, I would like to explain to you, not only how to get to the first measure of faith that saves you, but also how to get to the measure of faith that changes you as well. To do this, we will look at the most important chapter on faith in the Bible—Hebrews 11. This chapter is sometimes referred to as the "Hall of Faith". It discusses the great measures of faith of key people in the Bible.

We will discuss three verses and three people who, in my estimation, had three types of faith. Not three measures, measurements will be discussed shortly, but rather, three types of faith. Each of these is a type of faith that proved a measure of confidence in the coming Messiah. These three different types of faith led to each man's salvation. However, only one of the three men had a level of faith that God said "pleased" him. Let's take a look:

"By faith Abel offered unto God a more excellent sacrifice than Cain, by which he obtained witness that he was righteous, God testifying of his gifts: and by it he being dead yet speaketh. By faith Enoch was translated that he should not see death; and was not found, because God had translated him: for before his translation he had this testimony, that he pleased God. But without faith it is impossible to please him: for he that cometh to God must believe that he is, and that he is a rewarder of them that diligently seek him. By faith Noah, being warned of God of things not seen as yet, moved with fear, prepared an ark to the saving of his house; by the which he condemned the world, and became heir of the righteousness which is by faith."-Hebrews 11:4-7

In these familiar verses we see three men of faith—Abel, Enoch and Noah. All three had faith, but only one is singled out as having the testimony that he pleased God. Then, in the middle of the biographical sketches of these people of faith found in Hebrews 11, the writer stops and goes into an important dissertation on how to have a faith that pleases God. What made him go into this detail and why did he do it after describing the life of Enoch before returning to his biographical sketches? I think I have the answer.

In verse 4, we see God introduce us to a particular type of faith. It was a type of faith demonstrated by Abel. He offered to God an excellent sacrifice. Through this sacrifice he obtained witness (or proved to all spectators) that he was under God's control (that is to say righteous). This type of faith is what we would call WORSHIP. This type of faith is evidenced or observed by a form of worship. Abel's was only the second recorded sacrifice in Scripture, and all subsequent sacrifices in the Old Testament were intended to represent worship of God. Sacrifices were made under the influence of God for many different reasons, but they all represented a form of worship to God.

Therefore we can see that one type of faith that people express is found in worship. But worshipping more does *not* mean you have more faith. It simply means you are willing to express your current measure of faith more often than others. It's an indication of your appreciation for the faith you have, not of how much faith you have. Worship is a type of faith, but God does not record in the Scripture that this type of faith is what it "takes" to please Him.

I know a lot of people who are willing to express this type of faith. Some are willing to express their measure of faith in worship at least once per week. Some are willing to worship twice per week. Some people worship three times per week or perhaps even more. The good

Christians I know worship God in consistent fellowship with other believers in a good local church. However, there are other ways to express your faith, as well. Let's look at those:

Now in verse 7 we see a different type of faith expressed by Noah. It was not a form of worship; rather, it was a form of WORK. Noah worked for God. We read that "by faith Noah...prepared an ark." By doing this, he became heir of the righteousness that is by faith. Righteousness is being under God's control in Heaven (for justification) and on Earth (for sanctification). Heir means "to succeed in possession." Noah succeeded in possession of faith by having a confidence in God's promise to spare his family during a world wide flood.

He expressed his faith by following in obedience to what God had commanded. He worked and he worked hard. This does not tell us how much faith he had. It tells us how hard he was willing to

RIGHTEOUSNESS IS BEING UNDER GOD'S CONTROL IN HEAVEN (FOR JUSTIFICATION) AND ON EARTH (FOR SANCTIFICATION)

work in order to express his faith. His faith saved him, his work did not! But did his faith please God? We don't know because God doesn't record in these verses that he was pleased with Noah's faith.

I don't know about you, but I know a lot of people who are willing to express their current measure of faith through a form of work for God. As a matter of fact, the great Christians I know will express their faith in both WORSHIP and WORK. Yet, that type of faith doesn't necessarily please God.

In verse 5, we see Enoch expressed a type of faith that did please God. Let's review this verse: "By faith Enoch was translated that he should not see death; and was not found, because God had translated him: for before his translation he had this testimony, that he pleased God." Enoch's faith kept him from ever dying. His was a type of faith that, when he exercised it, pleased God. Based on God's response to it, I would say it pleased him incredibly! Enoch never died; he was taken body and all straight to Heaven.

Now this begs the question. What type of faith did Enoch have that made God comment on how pleased He was with Enoch? We simply must look at the few verses in the Bible that discuss Enoch:

"And Enoch lived sixty and five years, and begat Methuselah: And Enoch walked with God after he begat Methuselah three hundred years, and begat sons and daughters: And all the days of Enoch were three hundred sixty and five years: And **Enoch walked with God**: and he was not; for God took him."-Genesis 5:21-24

I think you probably have already seen his type of faith—Enoch WALKED with God. It's not clear if he did this his whole life, but this record shows that he did it at least from the time he had a son named Methuselah when he was 65. So from at least the age of 65 until his translation at the age of 365, the Bible records that Enoch walked with God and possibly before that. That's a possible 365 years of walking with God. Wow! And we struggle to walk with God for 365 days!

This type of faith is recorded in Hebrews as a faith that WALKED with God. Abel WORSHIPPED, Noah WORKED but Enoch WALKED. All three of those are good things, but it is the walking faith that pleased God. Enoch pleased God because He walked with God from the day he began his walk until he was taken to Heaven.

Now this makes sense. You cannot worship everyday, all day. You cannot work for God every day, all day. But you *can* walk with God every day, all day—and this is the type of faith that pleases God. I know people that will worship and I know people that work for God, but the best Christians I know are people that worship God, walk with God and work for God.

Most Christians are willing to worship, some more than others. Fewer Christians are willing to work, some less than others. But even fewer Christians are willing to walk with God, because a walk is intended to be a continual process, not to stop and start like our worship or work. We often want to express our faith by turning it on for church or for a sacrificial service opportunity.

But our faith goes inactive at other times, especially during times of adversity or during difficult circumstances in life. However, that is when we need our faith the most. And if we express faith during those trials, we will really please God. Yet, if we are not walking with God, we will not exercise our faith and we will fail in the midst of trial.

Those failures are the very things the devil uses to hinder your other expressions of faith—worship and work. How many people quit working in the church and then eventually they quit worshipping at the church because of discouragement over failure in their Christian lives?

Without a walk of faith, many will worship and some will work, but they will not be victorious. If your work is more important than your walk than you are performing (rather than transforming) into the image of a good man. However, if we will worship, then walk with

God and then work for God (as listed with Abel, Enoch, and Noah), we will find He is conforming us into the image of Christ.

When we fail in our Christian lives, often our response is to immediately run to find a way to serve or work for God to make up for our failure. Remember Adam? After he failed, he went to work making aprons of fig leaves. While Adam was busy working to relieve the guilt of his fall, God was wanting to go for a walk with him—but He couldn't find him!

What an accurate picture that is of many Christians. We *try hard to do better* by worshipping at church, but absent a sufficient walk with God, we fail. Rather than running to God for help, we find ourselves hiding from God and *working hard to feel better*. When we fail, we shouldn't focus on our work; we should focus on our walk.

Now this next truth is the heart of this whole chapter. It is found tucked away between the stories of Enoch and Noah. Notice, as I mentioned earlier, how God explains the different types of faith that Abel (worship) and Enoch (walk) and Noah (work) expressed. However, after describing Enoch's "God pleasing" walk, God detours the author into an explanation of Enoch's "faith pleasing walk." God explains that in order to have a *walk* that pleases Him, you must have a *faith* that pleases Him.

The measures of faith that provides a walk that will please God are the same measures of faith that will cause Him to dwell in our hearts, as taught in Ephesians 3. We can be sure that these measure of faith, once applied to our walk with God in **THUS YOUR FAITH IN GOD IS A MEASUREMENT OF YOUR CONFIDENCE IN GOD; BOTH IN WHAT HE HAS DONE (JUSTIFICATION) AND WHAT HE WANTS TO DO (BENEFICIAL SANCTIFICATION)** His Word, will cause the Lord to dwell within us continually. We have a precedent in the life of Enoch that this can continue from the time this measure of faith is experienced until the day we die (or 365 years, whichever comes first)! Let's look at these four measures so that we can learn how God intends for us to "register a full measure of faith."

"But without faith it is impossible to please him: for he that cometh to God must believe that he is, and that he is a rewarder of them that diligently seek him." -Hebrews 11:6

As we have defined previously, faith is a measurement of confidence. Thus your faith in God is a measurement of your confidence in God;

both in what He has done (justification) and what He wants to do (beneficial sanctification). We will look at the four measures of faith listed in Hebrews 11:6 as if they were inches on a ruler. Each measurement will be three inches in length. If we have a full measure of faith, it would metaphorically equal a foot of faith.

THREE INCHES OF FAITH—COMING TO GOD

The first three inch measurement of faith is a confidence in God that leads you to "come to God." Working with addicted adults and with troubled teens, I meet a lot of people that "come to God." They come to God every time they have a problem. But that's about all they do. Every time they need God, they come to Him. But as soon as they are bailed out of their immediate problem, they are gone again. When you come to God, you are sure to get closer to God, because if you draw nigh to Him, He will draw nigh to you. (James 4:8)

Now, God won't help someone who has no measure of faith, so if these people are intentionally trying to use God, it's unlikely He will help them. But if you come to Him in faith, He will not cast you out. People with this measure of faith may not have enough faith to stick around, but at least they have enough confidence in God to come to Him in times of urgent need.

I often have thought that God should punish people for behaving like this, but I guess that's why I'm not God. (So I guess I should start acting like Him!) You see, this measure of faith is not enough to save you. It's a level to gain God's goodness as He prepares you for repentance (Rom. 2:4), but absent of belief in Jesus, you remain unregenerated and unconfident in Him.

Thus, if God is going to be good to unbelievers in Jesus who come to God without Jesus, then I should consider doing the same thing and for the same reason. The reason is quite elementary—so that they can increase their measure of faith until they reach the second three inches and gain the 6 inches of faith necessary for salvation.

SIX INCHES OF FAITH—BELIEVE HE IS GOD

If we are patient with those who take advantage of God with their small measures of faith, they will eventually, over time hear enough of the Word to increase their faith. If they come to God, and come to God, and come to God, eventually you will probably find them believing that He is God. More importantly, they will believe in His Plan (Jesus Christ and Him crucified). This measure of faith brings salvation.

When you have this level of confidence in God and His Sacrifice you have six inches of faith. Remember, this is just a metaphor to show you where different types of people are spiritually in their faith. But faith that saves is not a full measure of faith. These people have the information, but they don't yet have the personal relation. Still, with six inches of faith out of twelve, they are half way there! Yet, unfortunately, that is where most Chrsitians begin to slow down.

NINE INCHES OF FAITH— BELIEVE THAT HE REWARDS DILIGENT SEEKERS

After they have acquired six inches of faith and have accepted the plan of salvation, new believers are given an opportunity to grow in their faith. They begin to attend functions and join classes at church. They start fellowshipping with other believers and as they observe those who are dynamic in their faith they see that God is rewarding them.

It doesn't take long for a new believer to realize that mature believers are indeed blessed by God. Whether they see someone donate a like-new car to a low paid godly school teacher, or they see people promoted at work that have less experience but are mature Christians, it's noticeable right away. God shows them these blessing in the lives of others so that they will be motivated to grow their faith to the next three inches of confidence. This level teaches that God rewards those who diligently seek Him.

This represents nine inches of faith. At this level you have heard, accepted and observed the truth. You lack only one more level. That is a level of participation. This level of participation is proof of your measure of confidence in God. Without this measure of confidence, you will not participate in the final three inches of faith—the twelve inches that "please Him."

TWELVE INCHES OF FAITH—DILIGENTLY SEEKING HIM

Most Christians that see God reward diligent seekers are content to be observers of this truth, rather than participants in it. Their faith, or their measure of confidence, is too weak to jump out and trust God for rewards in their own life. They know God rewards diligent seekers, but they seek to gain their own reward. However, as Christians, they are guaranteed by God to not gain their reward. They will seek it and never receive it.

They remain baby Christians because, while they believe God rewards diligent seekers, they won't participate in diligently seeking Him. Like newborn babies, they will grow as they are fed and exercised. Hearing the Word feeds a baby and doing the Word exercises it. If a baby eats and eats and eats without exercising they become nothing more than a fat baby! That's what we have in most of our churches—fat babies. They cry and whine and the only way they "get changed" is if someone else "changes them!" The reason for this is that after their birth they began to eat and failed to exercise.

A baby begins skinny until she is introduced to her mother's milk, then she gets fat. All of a sudden she starts crawling around, and then that baby fat disappears and she gets skinny again. Then her mother will introduce her to baby food and she will grow chunky again. By this time, however, she begins to walk and next thing you know she's back down to a skinny little thing.

Next, her mother will introduce her to solid food and back up in weight she goes, but she starts running and jumping and playing and she drops the pounds again. This cycle continues in our life until we reach about....oh, well. Let's say about 30 years old. Then what happens? We get fat. Why? Because we stop exercising!

This same truth can be applied to why most people never grow in faith much deeper than six or nine inches. They are so close to gaining the entire foot that would cause them to be filled with the Love of Christ, but they fall short. Why do they do this? Because they will not exercise their new found faith.

Diligent seeking of God in anticipation of a reward is your faith in ACTION!! Faith without works does not produce life, much less reproduce it! You will not be effective as a believer if you do not put your faith in action. You must worship to be informed of God, walk to have a relationship with God, and work in order to be used by God.

But each of these takes confidence. This confidence is not in your worship or your work, but rather in your walk. Paul tells us in Galatians 2:20, "And the life that I now live in the flesh, I live <u>by the faith</u> of the Son of God." In order to live the crucified Chrsitian life, you will need to have the full measure of faith. Come to God, believe in God, realize that He will reward your diligent seeking, and then seek Him diligently.

In conclusion, what does diligent seeking mean? Diligence means "constant in effort." Seek means "to go in search for." To diligently seek God, we must be constant and consistent in our efforts to go in search for Him. We need to know God intimately. That intimacy comes from a willingness to seek His face and an desire for our relationship with Him to be personal. Psalm 9:10 says, "And they that know thy name will put their trust in thee: for thou, LORD, hast not forsaken them that seek thee."

For Christ to dwell in our hearts, we must place Him there through meditation (chapters 1-4) and to keep Him there we must increase our faith (chapters 5-9). In order to have faith, real faith that will cause Christ to dwell in your heart and for you to be strengthened in the inner man, we will conclude our study in behavioral modification by reminding you of one final truth—that you will have to give up your ownership. "Yet not I, but Christ liveth in me!"

chapter nine

RELINQUISHING SELF-OWNERSHIP TO GOD

THE FINAL STEP NECESSARY TO STRENGTHEN OUR FAITH IS TO RELINQUISH SELF-OWNERSHIP TO GOD. PAUL WROTE, "I LIVE BY THE FAITH OF THE SON OF GOD, WHO LOVED ME, AND <u>GAVE HIMSELF FOR ME</u>."

Jesus Christ gave Himself for me. He did not make that sacrfice for me to be me, but for me to be Him. If I give someone $10,000 for a car, I do not give it so the car can have some spending money. I give it so the car will belong to me and take me wherever I want to go. The same is true with Christ's gift. He gave His life to take ownership of us.

The last step of faith is to relinquish our ownership of what we want to do, be and have. Those are the things of this world, and we are no longer of this world but have been chosen out of this world. (John 15:19) We have given Him our hearts by being reborn, and now we must submit our lives to Him, also. As we saw in chapter five, we know that without God's power, we cannot gain freedom in Christ.

We have tried to work out our problems, but we just can't do it. The key is to overcome our sinful habits by the power that is within us—the power of the Holy Spirit. Remember, Philippians 4:13 says, "I can do all things through Christ which strengtheneth me." We must yield our "rights" to Christ and let Him work through us to overcome our sinful habits.

A key passage that explains the truth of relinquishing self-ownership is found in 1 Corinthians 6:19-20. "What? know ye not that your body is the temple of the Holy Ghost which <u>is in you</u>, which ye have of God, and ye are not your own? For ye are bought with a price: therefore glorify God (or, make Him look good) in your body (or, your outward actions), and in your spirit (or, your inner man), which are God's."

The truth of relinquishing self-ownership reminds us of who we are and why we are here. Jesus Christ gave His body to redeem us and His Spirit to guide us. We are His, inside and out! The impetus of this knowledge should be a constant motivation for us to continually make God look good.

Now let me warn you that as you relinquish our lives to the Lord and begin to see victories, Satan is going to work that much harder to get you to doubt your abilities to serve God. The devil sees your spiritual growth, also. He is going to do everything he can to mess up the new path you are trodding—the new seeds you are sowing.

If the devil is not attacking you, then there is something wrong in your life! Any growth on your part will attract the attention of the devil. He is the Great Deceiver, and he knows how to sneak into your life. He knows your weak spots. Therefore, you need to continually be relinquishing self-ownership to God to keep the devil from gaining any victory in your life.

If you make a mistake, you can remain confident that God is still going to finish what He started in you. Philippians 1:6 says, "Being confident of this very thing, that he which hath begun a good work in you will perform it until the day of Jesus Christ." God is going to complete His work in your life!

The key to harmony with God is submission. It is the very basis of all five R's of Faith. Don't try to make excuses for your struggles. Just determine that if God says something is wrong, it is wrong–submit to Him! That is why we were crucified with Christ. That is why His Spirit lives within us. That is why we must exercise our faith in willing submission to His leading. Making God look good makes us look good. You are dead. Nevertheless, you live! To live like Christ, you must act like a dead man!

In conclusion, we see that our verses in Ephesians for Section Three teach us that we will be strengthened in our inner man and be filled with all the fullness of God if we place Christ within our hearts and cause Him to dwell there by faith. Thus we need to remember that we will memorize in our heads, but we will meditate in our hearts. So, we must manage what we meditate on.

Your chances are much better if you choose thoughts of meditation as God leads during your morning Journal time. Once you have your meditations for the day, use them, by faith to overcome all the circumstances in life. When you do, you will see, through the ensuing victories, that your faith is growing and your mind is stayed on Him. **Let's review the six steps for walking in the inner man.**

1) Take the acquisition of information to produce justification.
2) Study the Word of God to develop your personal relation.
3) Allow Spirit-prompted information to become your memorization.
4) Use your memorization as information for meditation.
5) Allow that meditation to develop your personal relation!
6) That personal relation will be the catalyst for you to enjoy the benefits of sanctification. I say this with great, well...shall I say ANTICIPATION!

Please reread our key verses one more time:

"That he would grant you, according to the riches of his glory, <u>to be strengthened </u>with might by his Spirit <u>in the inner man</u>; That <u>Christ may dwell</u> in your hearts <u>by faith</u>; that ye, being rooted and grounded in love, May be able to comprehend with all saints what is the breadth, and length, and depth, and height; And to know the love of Christ, <u>which passeth knowledge</u>, (information about God!) that ye might be filled with all the fulness of God."-Ephesians 3:16-19

And now, in conclusion, read the two verses that follow our key verse: Ephesians 3:20-21 "Now unto him that is able to do exceeding abundantly above all that we ask or think, according to <u>the power that worketh in us, </u>Unto him be glory in the church by Christ Jesus throughout all ages, world without end. Amen."

Remember, the power to do the impossible is found WITHIN you! This is the abundant Christian life. Everything else is the redundant Christian life. Exchange the devil's system of management for God's, and enjoy the exchanged life and intimate relationship He has planned for you! That is the foundational truths of behavior modification!

MORE BOOKS BY STEVEN B. CURINGTON

NEW RELEASE

THE UMBRELLA FELLA
(Code: CE-123 Price: $12.00)

Within every believer's heart is a desire to be all that God would have us to be. But, how can we be what God wants us to be, when we cannot even do the things God wants us to do?! The Umbrella Fella will help us understand our position in the Kingdom of Heaven's chain of command. Once we understand our position, it will forever change our disposition. It all begins with a two letter prepostion, the little word, IN.

NEW RELEASE

TODAY I LAY (Code: CE-124 Price: $8.00)

Seldom does a day go by that we are not faced with opportunity the to die to self. Most every believer recognizes their personal responsibility to put their own wishes and wants on the altar and to sacrifice himself for the cause of Christ.

However, God expects much more than a daily dying to self in order to qualify for the power of His ressurection. For us to experience this supernatural power on our lives, we must be willing to not only die for Christ, but to die with Him, be buried with Him and then be raised to walk with Him as we engage in a regular evaluation of our DBR.

NEVERTHELESS I LIVE
(Code: CE-100 Price: $18.00)

This commercially popular book written by Bro. Curington, should be a primary resource for educating you, your students, and your workers on the RU methods for "Living Freely in a Bound World." It is also the textbook for the Reformers Unanimous Addictions Program. You can also hear the Reformers Unanimous textbook read aloud with the new MP3 audio disc of this popular book.

order online **www.reformu.com** or call **815.986.0460**

WHY IS EVERYBODY CRYING
(Code: CE-118 Price: $7.00)

Most every Christian understands that they cannot be possessed. But yet they still find themselves doing things that make them sure the devil made them do it. How does this happen? Very simple...demonic oppression. Learn how Satan uses outside pressure (oppression) to render God's people discouraged and apathetic in their God-given responsibilities in life.

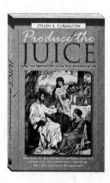

PRODUCE THE JUICE (Code: CE-121 Price: $16.00)

Bro. Curington's newest book Produce the Juice references the motivational stimulation that a gifted believer experiences when the Holy Spirit exercises His gift(s) that He has placed within the believer. In this book Brother Curington shows how using your gift produces great joy and excitement in the life of a believer. (Comes with a spiritual gifts test CD)

JOURNALS AND CURRICULUM

HOME DISCIPLESHIP COURSE
(Code: CE-098 Price: $59.00)

Behavior modification is needed by many people struggling from the results of conflicts and injuries obtained in today's society. This modification is not only needed because of the injuries but also the insults that we have added to those injuries in the form of addictions. This material written by the Founder of Reformers Unanimous is a biblical approach to overcoming both the insults and the injuries that so many are in bondage under. Follow the path that has set thousands free from bondage.

"IT'S PERSONAL" DAILY JOURNAL
(Code: CE-111 Price: $15.00)

The 90-day It's Personal Daily Journal is a proven method for developing a dynamic love-relationship with Jesus Christ. The journal is our #1 selling product in America! It comes complete with a CD explaining how to use the journal and its five forms of communication with God. (Classic size - 7 x 8 1/2)

COMPACT SIZE -"IT'S PERSONAL"
DAILY JOURNAL (Code: CE-112 Price: $12.00)

Same classic journal, but in a new compact size! It fits easily into your purse or Bible cover. This 5" x 7" journal contains all five forms of communication. (30-day supply)

ADULT FULL SIZE- "IT'S PERSONAL"
DAILY JOURNAL (Code: CE-116 Price: $17.00)

A larger version of our 90-day It's Personal Daily Journal is a proven method for developing a dynamic love-relationship with Jesus Christ. The journal is our #1 selling product in America! It comes complete with a CD explaining how to use the journal and its five forms of communication with God. (Full size - 8 1/2 x 11)

"IT'S PERSONAL" DAILY JOURNAL
(FOR YOUNG MEN) (Code: TC-104 Price: $15.00)

A 90-day supply of our very popular "It's Personal" Daily Journal for young teen men. Our "Daily Devos" help young men use the "pause and prompt" system to stimulate their God and I time into something very personal. It includes an instructional CD and a semester daily calendar, to-do list, daily med's (meditation) and memory cards, and the five daily forms of communication necessary to develop a dynamic personal walk with Jesus Christ.

"IT'S PERSONAL" DAILY JOURNAL
(FOR YOUNG WOMEN) (Code: TC-105 Price: $15.00)

A 90-day supply of our very popular "It's Personal" Daily Journal for young teen ladies. Our "Daily Devos" help young ladies use the "pause and prompt" system to stimulate their God and I time into something very personal. It includes an instructional CD and a semester daily calendar, to-do list, daily med's (meditation) and memory cards, and the five daily forms of communication necessary to develop a dynamic personal walk with Jesus Christ.

WALKIE TALKIE JOURNAL
(Code: KZ-111 Price: $8.00)

Children learn not only how to walk with God but to talk with God as well. This children's journal is formatted so that children can easily understand and complete it on their own. It includes an instructional CD for the child.

A STEVEN B. CURINGTON READING GUIDE

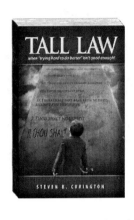

Living free in society.

Dealing with outside
pressure properly.

Gaining God's power
on your life.

Developing motivation to
do more for God.

Learning to decrease that
He might increase.

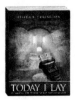